HOME BUILDING

After Tax Reform

Prepared by:
Economics, Mortgage Finance, and Housing Policy Division
National Association of Home Builders
Washington, D.C.
November, 1986

Additional copies of this report are available through the NAHB Bookstore:
$10.00 for members; $12.50 for non-members.
Address orders to:
NAHB Publications Orders
National Association of Home Builders
15th and M Streets N.W.
Washington, D.C. 20005

Copyright © 1986 by the
National Association of Home Builders of the
 United States
15th and M Streets, N.W.
Washington, D.C. 20005

No part of this book may be reproduced or utilized in any form or by any means, electronic or mechanical, including photocopying and recording, or by any information storage and retrieval system without permission in writing from the publisher.

ISBN 0-86718-285-7

HOME BUILDING AFTER TAX REFORM:
A BUILDER'S GUIDE

TABLE OF CONTENTS

Page

Preface

Chapter 1
The Homeowner Market   1

    Tax Provisions Affecting Homeowners
    Impacts on the Homeowner Market
    Overall Impact on Housing Starts and Property Values
    Related Issues

Chapter 2
Impacts on Rental Housing Development   11

    Taxes and Rental Housing
    Rental Housing After Tax Reform
    Market Adjustments
    Impacts on Projects Under Development
    Existing and Low-Income Projects

Chapter 3
New Constraints on Rental Investment   21

    Passive Loss Limitation
    Investment Interest Limitation
    At-Risk Rules
    Individual Minimum Tax
    Corporate Minimum Tax

Chapter 4
New Approaches to Rental Finance   37

    Participating Loans
    Changing the Debt to Equity Ratio
    Use of Zero Coupon Bonds
    Master Limited Partnerships
    General Observations

Chapter 5
The New Rules for Housing Finance   43

    Changes in Tax-Exempt Financing
    Builder Bonds
    Thrift Institutions
    Multiple Class Mortgage Securities

	Page
Chapter 6 **The Low-Income Rental Housing Credit**	57

    The Basics of the Credit
    Details on the Credit
    The Economics of the Credit

Chapter 7 **Commercial Real Estate and Historic Rehabilitation**	73

    Major Provisions Affecting Commercial Real Estate
    Rehabilitation Tax Credits

Chapter 8 **Second Homes, Resort Property and Land Development**	77

    Second Homes as Personal Residences
    Second Homes as Rental Properties
    Mixed Personal and Rental Use
    Installment Sale of Resort Property
    Land Development

Chapter 9 **Other Provisions Relevant to Real Estate**	83

    Installment Sales
    Corporate Distributions
    Miscellaneous Accounting Provisions

Chapter 10 **Adapting Real Estate Businesses to the Tax Reform Act of 1986**	87

    General Strategies
    Pre-1987 Tax Planning
    Post-1986 Considerations

Appendix **Provisions of the Tax Reform Act of 1986 Related to Housing**	95

PREFACE

The dust is beginning to settle after an unprecedented round of changes to the Internal Revenue Code. Even the Code itself has a new name--the Internal Revenue Code of 1986. For those who stayed out of the tax reform fracas of the last two years, now is the time to put on the reading glasses and catch up on the final results. For those who attempted to follow every twist and turn of the legislative process, now is the time to get out the magnifying glass to look for the many surprises that appeared at the last moment.

No matter what your involvement in the building business, there are important changes in store for you. Builders, investors, lenders, and even homeowners need to consider what the new tax system means to them and how to adjust the ways that they operate.

The new tax system poses challenges and presents opportunities in both the short and long terms. There are some actions you can take by the end of 1986 that may save you thousands of dollars in taxes. For example, before 1987 you should carefully consider:

* Selling appreciated property.

* Electing to have a "C" corporation taxed as a Subchapter S corporation.

* Disposing of or refinancing installment obligations on earlier sales.

* Paying for installation of utility services by a regulated public utility

* Obtaining certificates of occupancy on completed portions of rental projects.

When developing strategies for the longer term, a number of new pitfalls and opportunities need to be recognized. The pitfalls include:

* Less favorable tax treatment of installment sales of dealer or investment property.

* Tougher individual and corporate alternative minimum taxes.

* New stringent passive loss limitations.

* New restrictions on homeowner and multifamily tax-exempt financing.

The new opportunities include:

* Tax credits for construction, rehabilitation, or acquisition of low-income housing.

* New methods of raising mortgage funds through Real Estate Mortgage Investment Conduits (REMICs).

The Tax Reform Act of 1986 also changes the structure and functioning of all the markets in which builders operate, including land development, the starter-home and trade-up markets, the residential rental and commercial real estate markets, and the housing finance system.

All of these and many other topics are covered in this guide to the new tax law. While there is no perfect substitute for a close reading of the law and consultation with your tax advisor, we think that this guide will give you a good grounding in the post-tax reform rules of the game and help you develop strategies for operating in the new environment. We hope that you can profit from this knowledge by avoiding the pitfalls and seizing the opportunities created by the Tax Reform Act of 1986.

David F. Seiders
Senior Staff Vice-President
  for Economics, Mortgage Finance,
  and Housing Policy

CAUTION: The principles, suggestions, and conclusions set forth herein are based entirely on each author's reading of the recently enacted Tax Reform Act of 1986. Related regulations and rulings, together with judicial interpretations, may change these readings. No attempt has been made herein to evaluate the effect or impact of any state or local statutes or regulations that would apply in similar situations or circumstances. Accordingly, the material contained herein SHOULD NOT be utilized or applied to your operation without first consulting with your attorney and/or tax advisor.

Chapter 1

THE HOMEOWNER MARKET

Daniel N. Chambers
Housing Policy Analyst
National Association of Home Builders

The Tax Reform Act of 1986 will impact homeowners and the market for single-family homes in several ways. While the major homeowner tax deductions, for mortgage interest and property taxes, are preserved, the reduction in tax rates will diminish the tax advantages of becoming a homeowner or trading up to a more expensive house. Furthermore, there are new restrictions on tax-exempt financing and a phase-out of the tax advantages of builder-bond financing. These diminished tax incentives may cause a slight drop in homeowner demand and, thus, housing starts and property resale values in the short run, but, basically, the homeowner market is only moderately affected by the Act. (Single-family builders also should consult Chapter 5 on housing finance issues; Chapter 8 on second homes and land development; and Chapter 10 on how to organize their businesses.)

TAX PROVISIONS AFFECTING HOMEOWNERS

Exhibit 1.1 summarizes the provisions that affect homeowners, and groups them into general provisions, homeowner tax deductions, and special provisions which affect the market for new homes. The cumulative effect of all of these changes is a general reduction in the tax incentives for owner-occupied housing.

General Provisions

Personal Tax Rates. The overriding objective of this round of tax reform has been the reduction of marginal tax rates. For individuals, the Act replaces the present structure of 14 tax brackets--ranging up to a 50 percent rate--with two statutory rates, 15 percent and 28 percent, and a third effective rate of 33 percent. Exhibit 1.2 shows the taxable income levels corresponding to these new tax rates for the three filing statuses. The 15 percent and 28 percent rates first apply in 1988.

There will be "blended" rates in 1987 that are higher than for 1988, but still represent a rate cut from prior law. At moderately high income levels, households must pay an additional 5 percent of income in tax, until the benefit of being taxed at 15 percent on a portion of income is eliminated. This means that households with taxable incomes in the phase-out range face an effective marginal tax rate of 33 percent. (See below for an illustration of this phase-out.)

The cut in tax rates is not uniform across income levels. The largest reduction occurs at the highest income levels, although significant reductions occur at most income levels, especially in percentage terms. Exhibit 1.3 illustrates the tax cuts contained in the Act for 1987 and 1988.

Exhibit 1.1
Major Provisions Affecting Homeowners

General Provisions	Prior Law	1986 Tax Reform Act (when fully effective)
Personal Tax Rates	14 Brackets 11%-50%	2 Brackets 15% & 28% with phase-out of 15% rate (eff. rate of 33%)
Personal Exemption	$1,080	$2,000 but phased out at high incomes
Standard Deduction	$2,480 single $2,480 head of household $3,670 joint	$3,000 single $4,400 head of household $5,000 joint
Deduction for:		
State and Local Income & Personal Property Taxes	Yes	Yes
Sales Taxes	Yes	No
Other Personal Interest	Unlimited	None, except for qualified educational and medical expenses, if borrowed against home equity
Homeowner Deductions		
Homeowner Interest:		
Primary Residence	Yes	Yes
Second Home	Yes	Yes
Property Taxes	Yes	Yes
Provisions Affecting Home Builders		
Mortgage Revenue Bonds	Yes; 1987 Sunset	Yes; new volume and income restrictions; 1988 sunset
Builder Bonds (Installment Sales Treatment)	Yes	Severely restricted
Contributions in Aid of Construction	Not taxed	Taxed

Exhibit 1.2
Personal Tax Rates, Exemptions and Standard Deductions Under The Tax Reform Act

PERSONAL TAX RATES

1987 Taxable Income

Tax Rate	Married, Joint*	Head of Household	Single
11%	$ 0–$ 3,000	$ 0–$ 2,500	$ 0–$ 1,800
15	$ 3,000–$28,000	$ 2,500–$23,000	$ 1,800–$16,800
28	$28,000–$45,000	$23,000–$38,000	$16,800–$27,000
35	$45,000–$90,000	$38,000–$80,000	$27,000–$54,000
38.5	$90,000+	$80,000+	$54,000+

1988 Taxable Income

Tax Rate	Married, Joint*	Head of Household	Single
15%	$ 0–$29,750	$ 0–$23,900	$ 0–$17,850
28	$29,750+	$23,900+	$17,850+
Phase-outs begin (eff. 33% rate)	$71,900	$61,650	$43,150

PERSONAL EXEMPTION

1986 (prior law)	$1,080
1987	$1,900
1988	$1,950
1989	$2,000
1990+	$2,000 indexed to inflation

STANDARD DEDUCTION

	Married, Joint*	Head of Household	Single
1986 (prior law)	$3,670	$2,480	$2,480
1987	$3,760	$2,540	$2,540
1988	$5,000	$4,400	$3,000
1989+	The respective 1988 amounts indexed to inflation		

*For married individuals filing separately, the taxable incomes and standard deductions are one-half of the married, joint amounts.

Personal Exemptions. Another key feature of the Act is the near doubling of the personal exemption, from $1,080 now to, eventually, $2,000 in 1989 (see Exhibit 1.2 for the phase-in schedule). As with the benefit of the 15 percent tax rate, the entire personal exemption is phased out at higher income levels by employing a 5 percent surcharge to taxable income. This phase-out commences at the income level where the 15 percent rate phase-out ends, thus extending the range over which households face a 33 percent tax rate.

For example, a married couple filing jointly with one child pays a marginal tax rate of 15 percent up to $29,750 taxable income, where the 28 percent bracket begins. At a taxable income of $71,900, for every dollar of additional taxable income, the household pays the 5 percent surcharge on top of the 28 percent rate until the benefit of the lower 15 percent bracket is eliminated, which occurs at $149,250 taxable income. Then, the 5 percent surcharge is used to reduce the benefit of the three exemptions, which, in this case, is eliminated at $182,850 taxable income. After $182,850 taxable income, for this example, the 28 percent rate resumes on additional taxable income, and the household no longer has any deductions for personal exemptions. Exhibit 1.3 illustrates the return back down to the 28 percent rate; it should be emphasized that this "kink" occurs at different taxable income levels for different numbers of exemptions.

Standard Deduction. The Act also significantly raises the standard deduction as shown in Exhibit 1.2. The standard deductions and the tax brackets are indexed to inflation beginning in 1989; indexing of the personal exemption begins in 1990.

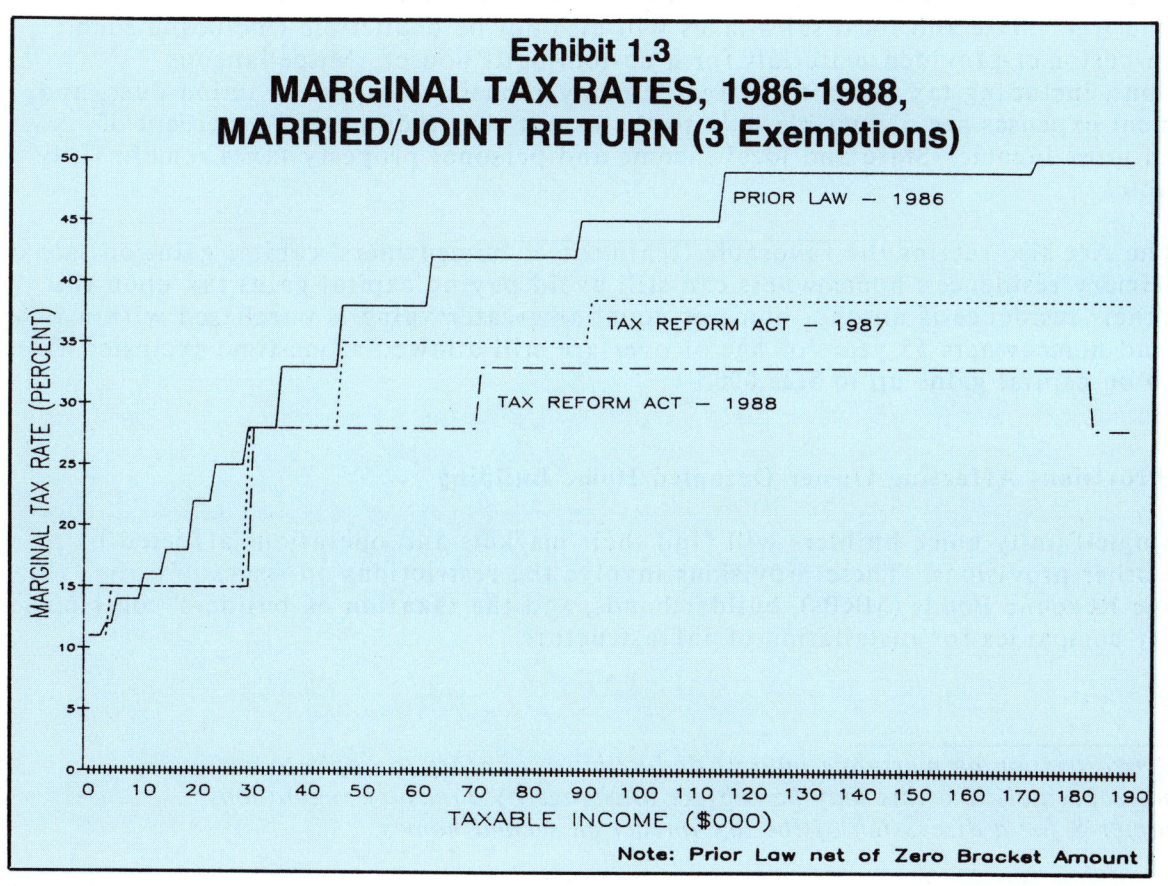

Homeowner Deductions

Two major housing expenses for homeowners--mortgage interest and real property taxes--remain deductible. Real property taxes are fully deductible, but there are some restrictions on the deduction for mortgage interest. In general, interest is deductible on a mortgage on a first or second home to the extent that the debt does not exceed the purchase price plus the cost of improvements of the respective home.* An exception is made for mortgage debt incurred to cover qualified medical and educational expenses, as long as the total debt does not exceed the "fair market value" of the residence. In addition, interest on mortgages may be deductible if the funds are used for investment purposes, subject to the limitation on investment interest.

Such a tight lid on borrowing against accumulated home equity would have impacted thousands of homeowners who have refinanced beyond the initial cost of their homes. Thus, an exception is made for interest on outstanding debt secured by the taxpayer's principal or second residence, if incurred on or before August 16, 1986. Such interest remains deductible (if the mortgage amount is below fair market value of the house), regardless of the purpose for which the borrowed funds are used. In general, it appears that this higher debt amount henceforth will be that taxpayer's cap on the mortgage debt which can generate deductible interest. Unfortunately, some homeowners were caught in the process of refinancing beyond this amount without any real notice of this limitation or the effective date.

The interest on all other types of loans for consumer purchases is not deductible under the Act. State and local sales taxes will also not be deductible (including such taxes on customer-provided materials for a custom-built house). Miscellaneous deductions, including tax preparation fees, employee business expenses, union dues, and investment expenses are deductible only to the extent that they exceed 2 percent of adjusted gross income. State and local income and personal property taxes remain fully deductible.

The Act also retains the favorable treatment of homeowners' capital gains on sale of their primary residences: homeowners can still avoid paying capital gains tax upon the sale of their residence if another home of equal or greater value is purchased within two years; and homeowners 55 years of age or over are still allowed a one-time exclusion from taxation on capital gains up to $125,000.

Other Provisions Affecting Owner-Occupied Home Building

Single-family home builders will find their markets and operations affected by several other provisions. These provisions involve the restrictions on issues of Mortgage Revenue Bonds (MRBs), builder bonds, and the taxation of builders' contributions to utility companies for installation of infrastructure.

The new restriction on mortgage interest deductibility appears to apply to each residence separately, but this may be subject to change by Treasury regulations. See Chapter 8 for a discussion of the tax impact on second homes.

Mortgage Revenue Bonds. State and local housing finance agencies currently issue federally tax-exempt bonds to finance below-market-rate mortgages, mainly to first-time buyers of moderately priced homes. While the Act extends the sunset of the use of these Mortgage Revenue Bonds (MRBs) by one year to 1988, there are several tighter restrictions on MRB issues for 1987 and 1988. Foremost, MRBs will be subject to a new state-by-state volume limitation on certain private activity bonds, including MRBs and multifamily housing industrial development bonds. Under prior law, MRBs had a separate cap based on total state mortgage volume and did not compete with other tax-exempt uses. The new state limitation for 1987 is the greater of $75 per capita or $250 million. This overall volume cap would have been $21.9 billion in 1985 and would have permitted less than 40 percent of the $55.7 billion in the private activity bonds actually issued in 1985.

Most importantly for new-home builders, there are stricter targeting requirements for the use of MRB funds, including (1) a new restriction on recipient income such that it does not exceed 115 percent of the area or state median income (whichever is higher), and (2) a tighter limit on the purchase price of the residence such that it does not exceed 90 percent of the area's average (down from 110 percent). Exceptions are provided for "targeted areas."

States may also exchange some or all of their MRB authority for authority to issue Mortgage Credit Certificates (MCCs), which are federal tax credits to homeowners based on their mortgage interest costs. The Act raises the exchange rate from MRB authority into MCC authority, but also tightens the targeting requirements for MCCs to be the same as for MRBs. With the Act's lower tax rates, credits such as MCCs are generally preferable to interest deductions. However, since the credit is non-refundable, homeowners must have enough tax liability if they are to fully use the credit. (See Chapter 5 for more details and implications of the changes in tax-exempt financing.)

Builder Bonds. Many larger-volume builders have been able to use the installment sales method of reporting profits from home sales, thereby deferring the taxation of such profits. Under this mechanism, builders take back mortgages from home buyers and pay taxes on profits as the mortgage payments are made. These mortgages secure bond issues which provide cash to the builder. The Act increases the amount of profit which builders must report in the year of sale, based on the builder's debt to asset ratio. If a builder has few assets relative to the amount of builder bonds and other debt outstanding, all or nearly all of the profit must be reported in the year of sale.

Details on this provision and on the relevant transition rules are provided in Chapter 5. In general, the change in the installment method first begins in the tax year ending in 1987, for property sales after February 28, 1986. Limited transition relief, however, applies to home builders, which spreads out somewhat the immediately reportable profits from sales in 1986 through 1988. Specifically, the portion of profits from sales in 1986 (after February 28) and 1987, that are supposed to be reported for the tax year ending in 1987, are instead spread out evenly over the tax years 1987, 1988 and 1989, i.e., one-third each year. One-half of reportable profits from 1988 is deferrable until 1989. Beginning with tax years ending in 1989, the full percentage of profits is taxable in the year of sale according to the ratio of debt to assets. This transition rule is more valuable than it appears because deferrals to 1988 will benefit from the lower tax rates in 1988.

Contributions for Construction of Utility Infrastructure. Under prior law, when a builder contributes money or property to a regulated public (i.e., investor owned) utility company as an inducement for the utility to provide service (e.g., water, gas, or electricity), the utility does not have to pay tax on the money or property received. Under the new law, however, such "contributions in aid of construction" made to a regulated public utility after December 31, 1986, will be treated as taxable income to the utility. This provision will increase builders' development costs, because non-municipal utilities now will seek additional money from builders in order to satisfy the tax liability that results from a contribution in aid of construction. However, utilities will be able to depreciate those assets, generally over 10 or 15 years, so there will be some offset for them.

Depending on how the local utility reacts to this change, it may be worthwhile to accelerate payments for such infrastructure into 1986.

IMPACTS ON THE HOMEOWNER MARKET

The total impact of the Act on the production of owner-occupied housing can best be viewed through the impacts on key parts of the market, notably, first-time home buyers and the trade-up market.

First-Time Home Buyers

The Act reduces the tax benefits of becoming a homeowner in two ways. First, the tax savings per dollar of homeowner tax deductions (mortgage interest and property taxes) and other deductions will be smaller due to the reduction in tax rates. Second, the Act's increase in the standard deduction and the elimination or reduction of certain non-housing deductions reduce the advantage of itemizing deductions over taking the standard deduction and thus of becoming a homeowner instead of renting.

Clearly, tax advantages are not the only reason for buying a home, and most households will proceed to act as if nothing had changed. But the loss of these tax benefits could deter some from doing so, or at least delay them. The reason is clear from the first column of Exhibit 1.4: the reduction in homeowner tax savings. For three different households typical of first-time buyers, with incomes of $35,000 and home prices of $80,000, there are substantially less tax savings from becoming a homeowner under the Act than under prior law. In two of the cases, the drop in cash tax savings is over $100 per month.

On the other hand, most prospective first-time home buyers will receive significant tax cuts as renters and thus will receive a boost in after-tax (or disposable) income. The second column of Exhibit 1.4 shows these increases in annual disposable income for the three prospective first-time buyers. While these increases happen to be roughly equal to the lost tax savings, much of these funds will go for things other than saving for a downpayment or for house payments, so the net effect will still be a reduced ability or inclination for such renters to become homeowners.

Many first-time home buyers also have benefitted from below-market-rate loans financed by state and local government issues of tax-exempt Mortgage Revenue Bonds (MRBs). In 1985, there were $12.0 billion of issues, funding about 236,000 mortgages, most of these to first-time home buyers. With the tighter restrictions on MRB issues, more of these prospective homeowners will have to qualify for market-rate financing. The price and income restrictions will impact particularly the new-home market. Also, builders will no longer be able to offer below-market builder bond financing, which is commonly used with moderately priced housing suitable to first-time buyers.

Trade-Up Buyers

Current homeowners will experience some of the same shifts in housing incentives as prospective first-time owners. However, most current homeowners will not consider becoming renters, even if they move; homeownership has become an important part of their life-style. In addition, if the taxpayer is not at least 55 years old, the cumulative capital gains becomes taxable if the household becomes a renter for more than two years.

The most important reaction may be from homeowners who are planning to trade up (i.e., buy a bigger or higher-quality home). Those considering trading up will have a reason to reconsider how much to trade up or whether to move at all. The Act's lower tax rates reduce the share of additional housing costs covered by additional tax savings, resulting in an increase in the "marginal" after-tax cost of purchasing more housing. Exhibit 1.5 illustrates the increase in the cost of trading up for a typical household for various levels of adjusted gross income. The increase in marginal cost is greater for households with greater declines in marginal tax rates (see Exhibit 1.3). Notably, an adjusted gross income of $50,000 results in a negligible rise in marginal cost because taxable income for such a typical joint filer is at a level ($30,000) where the reduction in marginal tax rates is very small.

Exhibit 1.4
Change in Taxes and Homeowner Tax Savings For Prospective First-Time Home Buyers

	Change in Annual Homeowner Tax Savings*	Change in Renter's Disposable Income*
Single (1 exemption)	−$ 720	+$ 656
Married, One worker (3 exemptions)	−$1,349	+$1,442
Married, Two workers** (2 exemptions)	−$1,324	+$1,037

Note: Income = $35,000; House price = $80,000

*These figures are the dollar changes in tax savings and disposable income observed by replacing prior law with the Act; so a negative value means a lower level under the Act.

**Takes the two earner deduction under prior law; one spouse assumed to earn $20,000 and the other $15,000.

Exhibit 1.5
Increase in After-Tax Cost of Trading Up— Between Prior Law and Tax Reform Act

Adjusted Gross Income	Percent increase in After-Tax Marginal Cost of Housing
$ 40,000	8.2%
$ 50,000	0.6%
$ 60,000	5.6%
$ 80,000	11.1%
$100,000	14.9%
$150,000	14.2%
$250,000	19.4%

Note: Marginal cost of $1,000 additional home value, beginning at a value equal to twice income. Household is married couple filing joint return with 3 exemptions and takes average non-housing deductions. Tax rates for 1988 are used for the analysis.

Generally, though, as income rises, so does the reduction in marginal tax rates under the Act. Consequently, the rise in the cost of consuming more housing is greater for higher-income households. Exhibit 1.5 shows that marginal cost is about 15 percent higher under the Act than under prior law at the $100,000 income level and is almost 20 percent higher at the $250,000 income level.* These higher costs mean that the high end of the market clearly will have less tax incentive to trade up, and may cause higher-income households to scale back their consumption of more housing and also their bids for more desirable areas, impacting the market for luxury homes. Trading up involving moderately priced housing will be less affected by the Act.

On the other hand, the Act creates a new reason to trade up or at least to move to another house. Because of the restrictions on mortgage interest deductions, it may not be possible to deduct the interest on home equity loans (for consumer purchases) where the home has appreciated in value; if so, only moving to another house would allow the interest on a larger loan to be deductible.

OVERALL IMPACT ON HOUSING STARTS AND PROPERTY VALUES

The reduction in homeowner tax savings, through its impact on first-time and trade-up home buyers, may soften some parts of the single-family housing market. In addition, the restrictions on mortgage revenue bonds and builder bonds will further limit the ability of some prospective home buyers to buy homes, at least for a while. The ensuing reduction in housing demand from the increased homeowning costs could initially depress property values. However, in all of these cases, the actual responses are far from certain.

For example, there is some question about how fast current or prospective homeowners will recognize the changes in the market and in their taxes. Contributing to this delay in recognition are the phase-ins of the tax changes, particularly the tax rates. The full tax rate reductions will not be in effect until the tax year 1988. Thus, it may take several years before taxpayers fully respond to the new tax law and to the market changes it will bring.

Another uncertainty is the impact of the Act on interest rates. The rise in taxes on business investment and rental real estate investment should dampen the amount of both and cause a further drop in interest rates. However, some analysts think the fall in business investment already has come and has contributed to this year's decline in interest rates. Thus, any further rate declines from reduced investment demand may be very small.

Another factor affecting the homeowner market, in the longer run, is changes in the rental market. As is discussed in Chapter 2, the Act removes many of the tax incentives to produce rental housing. This will lead to a substantial short-term reduction in rental starts, which should result in a noticeable rise in market rents over the next few years. Rent rises will make owner-occupied housing more attractive to prospective first-time buyers.

The increase in after-tax marginal cost is slightly lower at $150,000 income than at $100,000 for this example because the marginal tax rate increases from 28 percent to 33 percent between the taxable income levels related to these levels of adjusted gross income.

RELATED ISSUES

Remodeling

The Act will not greatly affect the remodeling market. One reason is that the new restrictions on mortgage interest deductions do not apply to most home improvement loans. Since the debt limit for deductible interest includes the cost of improvements, any past or future loans for remodeling will be within the limit and will thus generate deductible interest. The non-deductibility of consumer interest gives homeowners a tax incentive to take out second mortgages, rather than consumer debt, to pay for home improvements.

While there is no restriction on interest deductions for remodeling loans, the Act's reduction in marginal tax rates does reduce the tax savings associated with such deductions. This means that the additional (or marginal) homeowner costs resulting from remodeling are higher under the Act than they are under prior law, just as they are for trading up. Thus, Exhibit 1.5 also quantifies for remodeling how the cost of additional housing is higher under the Act. On the more positive side, remodeling may become a more attractive alternative to trading up (through actually moving) for those who are deterred by the higher after-tax cost of trading up.

Capitalization of Production Costs

The Act contains an accounting change that will affect builders who inventory houses. This change concerns the timing and accounting of deductions for the costs incurred in producing inventory. Under prior law, all direct production costs--such as the cost of materials contained in the house or used during production--are "inventoried," i.e., deductible as business expenses when the house is sold, not when the costs are incurred. However, some indirect production costs need not be inventoried and are deductible as current expenses.

The Act lengthens the list of expenses which must be inventoried rather than currently deducted, by requiring most indirect production costs to be inventoried, as well as all direct production costs. This accounting change will delay the deduction for tax depreciation, current pension and fringe benefit costs, as well as an allocated portion of general and administrative costs. The financial magnitude of this change for builders is uncertain, but it clearly requires more cumbersome accounting procedures for costing housing inventory.

Information Reporting on Real Estate Transactions

The Act will require the reporting to the IRS of the gross proceeds of real estate transactions. This practice was previously not required under Treasury regulations and it was felt to be needed to avoid an under-reporting of capital gains. The primary responsibility for reporting this information is on the person who conducts the settlement (generally the closing attorney). If there is no person responsible for closing the transaction, the Act specifies a chain of responsible parties: first the mortgage lender, then the seller's broker, and finally the buyer's broker. For transactions involving none of these parties, Treasury regulations must specify how the reporting is to be done. The Secretary of the Treasury also has the authority to exclude certain transactions from reporting if such reporting would not be useful.

Chapter 2

IMPACTS ON RENTAL HOUSING DEVELOPMENT

Douglas B. Diamond, Jr.
Assistant Staff Vice President for Housing Policy
National Association of Home Builders

Rental housing development has prospered the last few years because of strong market fundamentals and because a variety of tax provisions have expedited the flow of both debt and equity funds into it. The Tax Reform Act of 1986 substantially modifies the tax provisions supporting rental housing development, leaving it much more dependent on rental income to attract investment. Because of this, rental housing development will slow until market forces, particularly in the form of higher rents, restore its profitability. The new law may also change the way development financings are structured (see Chapter 4).

TAXES AND RENTAL HOUSING

Prior law contained three key tax provisions that contributed to making rental housing development attractive: (1) accelerated depreciation, (2) rapid amortization of construction period interest and property taxes, and (3) a large differential between the tax rate on capital gains and the rate on ordinary income. These provisions combined to produce a significant amount of tax savings early on in the life of a project, just when the economic risks were greatest, and to assure that most of these tax savings would not have to be paid back at time of sale. They also softened the blow of high interest rates caused by high inflation by permitting the immediate write-off of all interest expenses while providing that appreciation in the value of the property due to inflation was not taxed at full rates. Thus the tax advantages available to rental housing under prior law acted to reduce the risks of new development, to facilitate the financing of large-scale developments, to maintain rental investment during times of inflation, and to significantly reduce the rents required to provide investors a competitive rate of return, adjusted for risk.

The availability of these tax savings to investors prompted the development of convenient mechanisms for pooling equity investments from many people through syndications. The prospect of significant return on investment from tax benefits alone reduced the need for reliance on the fundamental economics of the projects. This implied that projected rental income did not have to be as high as otherwise and that investor scrutiny of project economics in general may have been lessened.

The financing of many projects was further facilitated by the availability of tax-exempt industrial development bonds (IDBs) for multifamily housing. The tax exemption of the interest on these bonds permitted them to be sold at interest rates two percent or more under the rate for conventional financing. Despite the presence of a variety of additional issuance costs and restrictions on the incomes of tenants in a portion of the units, the bonds were a convenient and economical source of debt financing for many developers.

Exhibit 2.1
Major Provisions Affecting Rental Housing
(excluding special low-income housing provisions)

	Prior Law	1986 Tax Reform Act (when fully effective)		Prior Law	1986 Tax Reform Act (when fully effective)
Depreciation	19-yr., 175% Declining Balance	27.5 yr. Straight-Line	At-Risk Exemption	Yes	Only for third-party financing
Construction-Period Interest & Taxes	10 yr. Amortization	Depreciated	Tax-Exempt Bond Financing	No volume limits	Low volume limits, tighter income limits
Capital Gains	60% Exclusion (20% max. rate)	No Exclusion (28% max. rate)	Historic Rehab Tax Credit	25% with 1/2% basis adjustment	20% with full basis adjustment
Depreciation Subject to Recapture	Excess of declining balance over straight-line	Not applicable (No cap. gains exclusion)	Alternative Minimum Tax Rate	20%	21%
Passive Loss Limitation	None	Rental loss only deductible against rental or passive income (5 year phase-in); except $25,000 in losses allowed if active manager or $7,000 in credits (phased out at higher incomes)	Housing-Related Preference Items for Minimum Tax	Depreciation in excess of straight line Capital Gains Exclusion	Depreciation in excess of 40 years straight line All "passive activity" losses (during phase-in) Interest on private-purpose tax-exempt bonds Gain deferred by installment sale

Exhibit 2.2
Characteristics of Sample Rental Project

Number of Units	100	Tax Rate of Investor	50% under prior law 28% under Tax Act

Development Costs
  Structure
  Land
	$4,257,250
	3,757,250
	500,000
		Operating Expenses
		  (per unit per month)
			$150

Construction Period	1/1/87 – 12/31/87	Vacancy Rate	5%

Placed in Service	1/1/88	Economic Assumptions:
		  Annual Increases in Operating Costs
		  Annual Increases in Rents
		  Annual Increase in Resale Value
			
			5.0%
			3.5%
			3.5%

Financing: Debt
  Equity
  Interest Rate
  Loan-To-Value
  Required Rate of Return on Equity (After-tax)
	Conventional
	Syndicated Equity
	10.5%
	75%
	13.0%
		Expected Holding Period	10 years

RENTAL HOUSING AFTER TAX REFORM

The Act changes nearly every tax aspect of rental housing investment. The major changes for non-low-income housing are listed in Exhibit 2.1 and are covered in greater detail in the Appendix. They include:

* A drop from 9 percent to 3.6 percent in the first year depreciation allowance.

* Depreciation of construction period interest and taxes over the 27.5 years depreciable life.

* The elimination of any differential between capital gains and ordinary tax rates.

* Further restrictions on the issuance of multifamily tax-exempt bonds.

All of these provisions go to the heart of the previously available tax advantages to investing in rental housing. Together, they constitute a withdrawal of tax policy support for rental housing. Moreover, as part of a reaction against this past history of tax subsidy and in order to raise revenue by retroactively limiting those tax subsidies, a provision was added that would generally limit the deduction of losses on rental real estate against income from any source other than "passive activities" or rental real estate activities. The details of this limitation on passive losses are examined in Chapter 3, but the basic thrust is simple. The provision is intended to end the tax sheltering of ordinary salary or business income or income from ordinary taxable investments, such as stocks and bonds, even for investments entered into under prior law.

It is clear that the passive loss limitation will significantly reduce the return on investment for many recent investors. However, for several reasons, the provision may not be as significant as it appears for new investments. First, under the new rules, usually there will not be large losses in the early years of a rental housing investment, because of much lower depreciation allowances. Second, the new lower tax rates mean lower tax savings from taking the losses. Third, the foregone deductions are not lost forever, but only suspended until they can be taken against income from that or another passive investment. Last, the remaining suspended losses will be fully allowable at time of sale of the property. For all these reasons, the value of receiving those tax savings today rather than at time of sale is not very large.

Another major departure in the new law is the provision of a large tax credit for investment in low-income rental housing. The credit is analyzed at length in Chapter 6.

Impacts On A Typical Project

One way to understand how the 1986 Act alters the rental housing development business is to analyze in some detail a typical multifamily project. While the size and dollar figures on actual projects will vary across projects and around the country, the basic economics of this illustrative project should be similar to most projects. The analysis is based on the NAHB Simulation Model of a rental housing development, which calculates the present value of projected cash flows.

Exhibit 2.2 describes the project to be analyzed. It is of medium size (100 units), and the total development cost per unit, including land, is about $43,000. For simplicity, we assume construction is started on January 1, 1987 and the project is put in service with 95 percent occupancy exactly one year later. It is then sold ten years later. Meanwhile, operating expenses increase at the rate of inflation, assumed to be 5 percent, while rents and the resale value increase at only 3.5 percent. The project has permanent conventional financing with a 75 percent loan at 10.50 percent, amortized over 30 years. The equity of about $1 million is contributed fully in the first year by ten limited partners, who expect that a combination of tax benefits, net operating income, and capital gains will provide them a yield after taxes of 13 percent, i.e., a risk premium of about 5 percent over the return on high-rated tax-exempt bonds. All cash flows are discounted at the 13 percent internal rate of return.

When the project is analyzed under the old tax law provisions, the initial average rent required to meet investor expectations is only $418. Actual average rents on new projects nationwide are running only a little higher, about $430. This level of rent does leave a small amount of negative cash flow to be covered the first few years, requiring a partially deferred mortgage, a reserve, or other provision.

The cash flows for this project are displayed in Exhibit 2.3. The rents do not provide positive cash flow for seven years; thus most of the investor's return comes from appreciation and tax savings. The tax savings are significant. At the 50 percent tax bracket, the initial year loss of $385,000 generates total tax savings of $192,500, or $160 per unit per month. If rent-up had taken a significant amount of time, first-year losses would have been much larger.

The potential impact of a provision such as the passive loss limitation can be seen clearly at this point. The ten limited partners would each have a net loss of about $39,000 on the project. Taking that loss under the old rules would save them over $19,000 in taxes. Even after kicking in another $5,300 to cover negative cash flow, they would experience a 13.1 percent after-tax current return on their investment.

The passive loss limitation alone would cause the return available under prior law to be deferred until time of sale unless the investor has qualifying passive income to offset. That deferral would significantly reduce the value of the tax benefits. But the other provisions of the new law are even more devastating.

As shown in Exhibit 2.4, under the new depreciation rules, the reported first year loss is cut by over half and, under a 28 percent tax rate, the expected tax savings drop by about three-quarters. This drop in tax savings and the higher tax rate on capital gains are so significant that the passive loss limitation may not be a dominant concern.

This conclusion is reinforced by inspecting the bottom line of this project. The after-tax rate of return under the old law was set at 13.0 percent. If rental income remains unchanged, the return drops under the new law by two-fifths, to 7.6 percent, even if all losses are taken currently. If the passive loss limitation is

Exhibit 2.3
Cash Flows of Sample Rental Project: Prior Law

Year	Rent	Before-Tax Cash Flow*	Depreciation and Amortization	Tax Savings	Current Return**
1988	$419	($53,260)	$348,093	$192,532	13.1%
1989	434	(45,542)	318,402	172,938	12.0
1990	449	(37,688)	291,445	154,546	11.0
1991	465	(29,702)	266,970	137,222	10.0
1992	481	(21,585)	244,750	120,839	9.3
1993	498	(13,340)	224,577	105,284	8.6
1994	515	(4,971)	206,262	90,448	8.0
1995	533	3,519	189,633	76,232	7.5
1996	552	12,125	174,536	62,453	7.0
1997	571	20,843	172,411	42,221	5.9
Sale		$2,085,913		(923,481)	109.2

Internal Rate of Return: 13.0% After-Tax

*Includes operating income (loss) and mortgage principal payments.

**Tax savings plus cash flow divided by initial equity.

Exhibit 2.4
Cash Flows of Sample Rental Project: New Law

Year	Rent	Before-Tax Cash Flow*	Depreciation	Tax Savings	Current Return**
1988	$419	($53,260)	$136,627	$48,607	(0.1%)
1989	434	(45,542)	136,627	45,948	(0.0)
1990	449	(37,688)	136,627	43,197	0.1
1991	465	(29,702)	136,627	40,348	0.1
1992	481	(21,585)	136,627	37,395	1.5
1993	498	(13,340)	136,627	34,333	2.0
1994	515	(4,971)	136,627	31,153	2.5
1995	533	3,519	136,627	27,848	2.9
1996	552	12,125	136,627	24,410	3.4
1997	571	20,843	136,627	20,829	3.9
Sale		$2,085,913		(851,203)	116.0

Internal Rate of Return: 7.6% After-Tax
   6.9% After-Tax (Passive loss limit binding)

*Includes operating income (loss) and mortgage principal payments.

**Tax savings plus cash flow divided by initial equity.

binding, the return drops only a little further, to 6.9 percent. If rents rise sufficiently to restore the rate of return to 13 percent, our sample project will run only small tax losses. In that case the passive loss limitation will only matter for the rent-up period.

MARKET ADJUSTMENTS

Clearly, rental housing development will not come to a complete halt because of the changes wrought by the 1986 Act. The various players will instead begin an adjustment process which will take several years. In fact, it is likely that the market's adjustment to the 1981 Tax Act had not been completed by the time the 1986 Tax Act was being debated.

One of the first effects should be a sharp decline in the interest of investors in the tax shelter aspects of rental residential real estate. These tax advantages will be greatly diminished for new construction. In addition, most investors currently do not have sufficient qualifying passive income to fully utilize the remaining losses. One response commonly suggested is to reduce the leverage of projects, so that, implicitly, equity investors supplant some of the debt financing and receive a return on what is essentially a low-risk loan that is tax sheltered by the remaining depreciation allowances. In our sample project, a 50 percent loan-to-value ratio nearly accomplishes the goal of eliminating tax losses and yields an internal rate of return of 7.2 percent even at current rent levels.

This kind of return is not competitive for most equity investors in what is still a relatively risky endeavor. Reducing leveraging only partially compensates for the passive loss limitation and does nothing to compensate for the loss of rapid depreciation and capital gains treatment. The loss of tax advantages will have to be balanced primarily by increases in rent levels.

Thus the key to most future projects will be projected rent levels that provide most of the net returns to equity investors. Whether those rents are realistic depends heavily on the local market situation, including the potential for rent controls being applied. Markets with strong growth in rental demand and moderate-to-low vacancy rates may be able to support higher rent levels in the relatively short term. This prospect may be sufficient to keep up investor and lender interest in new projects. In fact, builder/developers who do not depend on outside investors may proceed based on the expectation that few others will build.

However, many markets are currently experiencing above-average vacancy rates and slow rent-ups. These markets may require several years of declining vacancy rates before rents can be raised sufficiently to support new construction. In the meantime, there may be declines in development costs, including land prices, which may make new development feasible earlier.

How much will rents ultimately need to rise? In the simplified project described above, a total jump of about 24 percent would be needed to bring the after-tax rate of return of investors back to 13 percent. However, there are several reasons to expect that the full increase may not be needed. Not only may land and other development costs go down, but interest rates may decline (and may have already declined) because of a general fall-off in business and residential investment due to the Act. In addition, other investors who do not require such high yields, such as life insurance companies, pension funds, and other institutional sources, may become debt or equity participants in more rental housing (see Chapter 4 for further discussion).

The journey back to a healthy rental housing development market will be a fairly long one, with the time frame varying widely across markets. One of the major uncertainties is how the small investors with one or more single-family, townhouse or condo units may respond, since such units make up over one-third of the rental stock overall. If few new investors wish to hold the units for rental after tax reform, the rental market may tighten up more rapidly.

Overall, a drop in new investment may mean that rents five years from now will be as much as 15 to 20 percent higher than they would have been. Despite this, an underlying demographic shift away from rental demand over the next 5-10 years could keep the rental development market soft for even longer.

OTHER IMPACTS ON DEVELOPMENT

One of the winners under tax reform may be the condominium market. There are three reasons for this prospect. First, once rents begin to rise significantly, interest in apartment ownership should be boosted. Second, the Tax Act eliminates the necessity that existed under prior law to sell a building to a converter in order to gain capital gains treatment on the sale. In the absence of a capital gains rate differential, owners will not suffer higher taxes from direct conversion. Third, condominium conversion within a limited partnership may be an attractive way to generate passive income, against which passive losses may be taken.

The Tax Act sets up some incentives to change some other aspects of rental housing investment. For example, taxes on capital gains tend to cause investors to defer the sale of a property, since the sale will cause them to lose a portion of their equity to taxes. Under prior law, this incentive was diminished by the special lower rate on capital gains combined with favorable recapture rules that treated the recapture of most depreciation as capital gains. In addition, a seller could take back financing, elect installment sales treatment, and thereby continue to earn a return on the portion of his equity that would have gone for taxes.

Under the new law, (1) there is no differential between capital gains rates and ordinary rates, (2) capital gains rates are generally higher than under prior law, (3) the value of installment sales treatment is diluted and (4) "burned-out" shelters provide passive income which can be sheltered by losses from more recent projects. Moreover, the tax advantage of renewing the depreciable basis is reduced. All of these factors will tend to cause owners to hold on to rental investments longer. Alternatively, owners may seek out tax-free exchanges more often.

Another shift which may occur is towards more ownership by moderate-income households, either as limited partners or sole proprietors. If rents rise as much as expected, rental investments will tend to generate taxable income, not tax shelter. The impetus towards upper-income interest in rental housing will be lessened, relative to middle-income investors. Also, middle-income investors who qualify as "active participants" will still be able to shelter up to $25,000 in income from non-passive activities, an amount that is quite significant at middle-income levels.

IMPACTS ON PROJECTS UNDER DEVELOPMENT

Most active developers have one or more projects which are falling into the gray area between the old law and the new law. The Act provides a number of transition rules which may or may not affect these projects and may overlap to create some unusual combinations of grandfathering.

In general, the new provisions of the law go into effect on January 1, 1987. For rental projects, this is the date before which they have to be placed in service to attain prior law treatment of depreciation and construction period interest and taxes. This date is extended to January 1, 1991 for property that is constructed or acquired pursuant to a written contract that was binding on March 1, 1986. The new at-risk rules apply to all property placed in service after 1986, whether or not there was a binding contract as of March 1, 1986. Obviously, everything posible should be done to meet the 12/31/86 deadline. Portions of projects may qualify for certificates of occupancy (and thus placement in service) even if the entire project is not complete.

The capitalization into the basis of construction period interest and taxes also goes into effect only after 1986. Thus all such payments made in 1986 will receive prior law treatment, and the timing of such payments should be carefully monitored and accelerated, if possible.

The passive loss limitation rules apply to all rental real estate after 1986, no matter what date it was placed in service. However, certain properties will qualify for a phase-in of the rule, such that only 35 percent of the excess losses and credits are disallowed in 1987, 60 percent in 1988, 80 percent in 1989, 90 percent in 1990 and 100 percent in 1991. The critical date for qualifying for this phase-in is the date of enactment of the bill, October 22, 1986.

To qualify, ownership had to be established on or before that date. However, a contractual obligation to purchase, even subject to certain contingencies outside the taxpayer's control, will qualify as an ownership interest. In general, the property must also had been placed in service by that date. However, this latter requirement is met if a binding contract to construct or acquire the property was entered into on or before August 16, 1986.

In addition to the change in the depreciation of real property, the depreciation of the personal property involved in a rental project (e.g., appliances) is also changed by the new law. In general, the depreciation of such property has been improved, but the investment tax credit was repealed (effective 1/1/86). A special rule permits applying the new depreciation on personal property to property placed in service after 6/30/86. Owners of buildings placed in service between 7/1/86 and 12/31/86 should consider electing this special treatment of associated personal property.

Chapter 3 and the Appendix provide additional details on these and other transition rules.

EXISTING AND LOW-INCOME PROJECTS

Rental housing investments established before 1987 will generally continue under prior law, with two key exceptions. Many such investments will be subject to the passive loss limitation, albeit on a phased-in basis. Second, the end of the capital gains rate differential means full recapture at ordinary rates of all depreciation at time of sale.

This turn of events is financially disappointing from the point of view of recent investors in existing projects. They may not be able to deduct fully all of the losses anticipated when the investment was entered into. Moreover, those losses that remain deductible under the phase-in rule will be against lower tax rates, and at time of sale, both the depreciation taken and any appreciation will be taxed at higher rates than expected at time of investment.

An analysis of these shifts through the NAHB Simulation Model of a rental investment suggests that, even though the project discussed above had been completed in 1986, the effective after-tax rate of return is cut from the 13 percent that would have been projected under prior law to 8.4 percent (assuming no change in projected rent levels). The drop is even sharper if the investor is impacted by the phase-in of the passive loss limitation. Of course, the longer the investment has been held prior to the new law, the smaller will be the impact on the total return. In any case, though, the resale value of the project after January 1, 1987 is 15-20 percent lower, even if rents are expected to rise by 20 percent over the next five years.

These results suggest that some properties may be worth less than their mortgages and are ripe for default. Undoubtedly, that is the case for properties that may have been close to default anyway. Whether or not other, more healthy projects will be pushed towards default will depend on the specific circumstances of the property and the investors, especially how much equity had been built up, how much recapture the investors would be subject to, and how much of a market there may be for the project among tax-insensitive investors such as life insurance companies, tax-exempt entities, or foreign investors. Of course, actual default and foreclosure depends greatly on the flexibility of the lender as well.

Even long-term owners of rental real estate will find their returns cut retroactively by the rise in the capital gains rate. For them, there are significant incentives to sell before the end of 1986. The ideal sale is from a long-time holder to an investor not significantly impacted by the passive loss limit and thus able to benefit from the 19-year depreciation available until December 31, 1986.

There has been discussion of whether limited partners in the middle of a pay-in process would find it advantageous to default on the rest of their contributions. Aside from the legal and credit ramifications of such an action, the economics are not as simple as it may first appear. Even if the return on the total investment will be less than alternative investments, the return must be analyzed from the perspective of only the remaining payments, excluding the earlier ones. Moreover, the cost of paying taxes currently on the amounts of depreciation already taken must be factored in. Finally, the prospects for rising rents must be considered.

Federally subsidized low-income housing projects are among the investments most likely to show an advantage to investor default. The reason is that, as investments, the tax benefits constitute most if not all of the anticipated economic returns. Because of these considerations, special relief from the passive loss limitation was provided to certain investors in low-income projects. In general, to be qualified, an investor must not have made half or more of his or her total required payments before 1987 (except for certain FmHA projects which need only to have 35 percent of the pay-in outstanding). See the Appendix for a number of other requirements and special rules for projects placed in service after August 16, 1986. In these cases, the investment is exempted from the passive loss limitation for a period up to seven years from the date of the original investment.

OTHER ASPECTS OF RENTAL RESIDENTIAL REAL ESTATE

The Chapters following this examine in more detail specific aspects of the new law with respect to rental housing markets. Chapter 3 describes the details of the passive loss limitation, the at-risk rule and other new constraints on rental investment. Chapter 4 suggests how the sources and types of equity funds may shift. Chapter 5 reviews the changes in tax-exempt financing. Chapter 6 analyzes the new tax credit for low-income housing. Chapter 7 covers markets in commercial real estate development, and historic and non-historic rehabilitation. Chapter 8 reports on second homes and resort development. Chapter 9 describes two important provisions with respect to the disposition of rental real estate. Finally, Chapter 10 examines how the business operations of a diversified builder might be reorganized in light of the new law.

Chapter 3

NEW CONSTRAINTS ON RENTAL INVESTMENT

Floyd L. Williams
Tax Counsel, Government Affairs Division
National Association of Home Builders

THE PASSIVE LOSS LIMITATION

In the Tax Reform Act of 1986 (the "new law"), Congress took direct aim at so-called "tax shelters" by eliminating the ability of individuals to deduct tax shelter losses against other income. Under prior law, one of the primary attractions of an investment in rental housing was that an individual could deduct net losses flowing from that investment against any other income without limitation. This, coupled with the ability to "leverage" an investment with nonrecourse debt, could provide significant tax losses with little current out-of-pocket cost. For example, assume an individual contributed 10x cash to a real estate limited partnership and assumed 90x of partnership nonrecourse liability (for a total basis in the investment of 100x). Assume, further, that the individual's share of the investment produced 10x of rental income and 40x of deductible expenses from a combination of depreciation deductions, interest expenses, and operating expenses. For his 10x cash investment, the individual was able to deduct 30x of losses against any other income (e.g., salary, dividends, interest, etc.). Under the new law, assuming this was the individual's only investment, only 10x of the 40x in expenses could be deducted currently. That is, the loss from the investment could "shelter" only the income from the investment.

The new law cracks down on "tax shelters" by providing new limitations on losses and credits derived from so-called passive activities. The passive activity loss limitation applies to individuals (including partners and subchapter S corporation shareholders), trusts, estates, closely-held subchapter C corporations, and personal service corporations. Notably, the limitation does not apply to regular subchapter C corporations.

Passive activities, for purposes of the loss limitation, include (1) any activity involving the conduct of a trade or business in which the taxpayer does not materially participate, and (2) any rental activity. However, "working interests" in oil or gas properties generally are not considered to be passive activities, provided that taxpayers do not have limited liability with respect to such interests.

A rental activity (which, by definition is a passive activity) may include the performance of services that are incidental to the activity (e.g., a laundry room in a rental apartment building). However, if a sufficent amount of incidental services are rendered in connection with a rental activity, those services may rise to the level of a separate activity. Alternatively, the entire activity may not constitute a rental activity for purposes of the passive loss limitation if the provision of services constitutes a dominant part of the activity (e.g., a hotel).

In the case of an activity other than a rental activity, a taxpayer may deduct losses without restriction if he materially participates in the activity. A taxpayer will be treated as materially participating in an activity only if he is involved in the operations of the activity on a regular, continuous, and substantial basis. In the case of a limited partnership interest, it is conclusively presumed that the taxpayer has not materially participated in the activity. However, the Secretary of the Treasury is given regulatory authority to provide that, in certain situations, limited partnership interests will not be treated as interests in passive activities, in order to prevent individuals from circumventing the passive loss restrictions by placing non-passive activities into limited partnerships.

In order to satisfy the material participation standard, the individual's activity must relate to the operations of the activity. An individual is most likely to have materially participated in an activity in cases where involvement in the activity is the taxpayer's principal business. By contrast, when an activity is not an individual's principal business, it is less likely that the individual is materially participating. However, the fact that an activity is or is not an individual's principal business is not conclusive in determining material participation. That is, an individual may materially participate in no business activities, or he may materially participate in more than one business activity.

For purposes of the material participation test, the performance of management functions generally is treated no differently than rendering other services or performing physical work with respect to the activity. However, a merely formal and nominal participation in management does not constitute material participation. Rather, a genuine exercise of independent discretion and judgment is required. The utilization of employees or contract services to perform daily functions in running a business does not prevent an individual from qualifying as a material participant. However, the activities of agents are not attributed to the individual. Thus, the individual must personally perform sufficient services to establish material participation.

If an individual is involved in a passive activity (i.e., either a business activity in which he does not materially participate or a rental activity), then neither a passive activity loss nor a passive activity credit is allowed for the taxable year. A passive activity loss is the amount (if any) by which the aggregate losses from all passive activities for the taxable year exceed the aggregate income from all passive activities for the year. Likewise, a passive activity credit is the amount (if any) by which the sum of tax credits from all passive activities allowable for the taxable year exceeds the regular tax liability of the taxpayer for the taxable year allocable to all passive activities. Thus, in general, losses and credits derived from passive activities may offset only income and taxes derived from passive activities.

It is important to note that the determination of passive activity losses and credits is made on an aggregate basis. Thus, income from passive activities may be reduced by losses from other passive activities. For example, assume that an individual has a net loss of 10x from his investment in rental housing and has net income of 10x from a "non-working" limited partnership interest in an oil and gas venture (or from any other business in which he is not a material participant). That individual would have neither passive income nor passive loss, since the passive loss "nets out" the passive income in this example.

Income from passive activities does not include "portfolio income," e.g. income from interest, dividends, annuities, or royalties not derived in the ordinary course of a trade or business, or gain or loss attributable to the sale of property held for investment (unless the investment property is a passive activity). Furthermore, neither salary income nor income derived from a non-rental business in which the taxpayer is a material participant is considered passive activity income. As noted above, this effectively eliminates the ability of an individual to "shelter" other income with losses derived from rental real estate or any other passive activity. Furthermore, the passive activity loss restriction adds significant complexity to the tax law because now individuals will have to keep track of, and differentiate between, different types of income (i.e., passive activity income, active business or salary income, and portfolio income).

Treatment of Portfolio Income

As noted above, the portfolio income of an activity (e.g., interest, dividend, royalty, or annuity income earned on funds set aside for future use in the activity) is not treated as passive income from the activity, but, rather, must be accounted for separately. Likewise, portfolio income of an entity that is not attributable to, or part of, an activity of the entity that constitutes a passive activity also is accounted for separately from any passive income or loss. For example, interest received on a reserve fund to pay for repairs and replacements to a low-income housing project would be treated as portfolio income and, thus, have to be segregated when calculating net passive activity income or loss from the housing project.

In addition, gain or loss from sales or exchanges of portfolio assets (including property held for investment) is considered to be portfolio gain or loss. However, for purposes of this rule, an interest in a passive activity is not treated as property held for investment. Portfolio income is reduced by deductible expenses (including properly allocable interest expenses) that are clearly and directly allocable to such income. Accordingly, those deductions are not treated as allocable to a passive activity. It is anticipated that the Treasury Department will issue regulations providing guidance to taxpayers with respect to interest allocations by December 31, 1986.

The Interest Deduction Limitation

Interest deductions that are attributable to passive activities are treated as passive activity loss deductions rather than investment interest deductions. Thus, those interest deductions are subject to restriction under the passive activity loss limitation and not under the investment interest limitation. Likewise, interest and losses from passive activities generally are not treated as investment income or loss in determining the amount of the investment interest limitation. However, any passive losses that are allowed under the phase-in of the passive loss limitation (other than losses from rental real estate activities in which the taxpayer actively participates) reduce net investment income for purposes of the investment interest limitation.

Excess Passive Activity Losses

As previously noted, losses arising from a passive activity may be deducted only against income from that or another passive activity. Excess passive activity losses for any year become, in effect, "suspended losses." These suspended losses are carried forward indefinitely (but are not carried back) and are allowed in subsequent years against passive activity income. Upon a taxable disposition of a passive activity, suspended losses are allowed in full. Assume that an individual's only passive activity is ownership of an apartment building. Assume, further, that for the current taxable year the building produces 10x of rental income and 20x of loss. The excess loss of 10x would become a suspended loss that would be carried forward to subsequent years and would be available for use against passive income in subsequent years.

If some passive losses from more than one activity are not deductible in any particular year, the amount of suspended losses from each passive activity is determined on a pro rata basis. For each separate activity, the portion of the loss that is suspended and carried forward is determined by the ratio of net losses from that activity to the total net losses from all passive activities for the year. Such an allocation is necessary in order to determine the cumulative suspended losses for any particular activity, which are then allowed in full upon a disposition.

This allocation rule is illustrated in the following example: Assume a taxpayer owns three rental buildings. He has $25,000 of net losses from building A, and $15,000 of net losses from building B. Building C produces $20,000 of rental income. The taxpayer can offset the $20,000 of passive income with $20,000 of passive losses. The $20,000 of remaining loss is suspended and is allocated as follows:

$12,500 to building A   ($20,000 net passive loss X $\frac{\$25,000}{\$40,000}$)

$7,500 to building B   ($20,000 net passive loss X $\frac{\$15,000}{\$40,000}$)

These suspended losses can be used to offset any net passive activity income in subsequent years. While the statutory language may not be entirely clear, it would appear that the cumulative suspended losses on each property will be reduced by the net passive income in proportion to their share of the total of suspended losses for all properties.

Dispositions

A fully taxable disposition of a passive activity triggers all suspended losses with respect to that activity. In order to trigger the loss, however, the taxpayer must dispose of his entire interest in the activity. Specific "ordering" rules apply with respect to dispositions of passive activities. Under these ordering rules, suspended losses of an activity are allowable as a deduction against income in the following order: (1) Income or gain from that passive activity for the taxable year (including any gain recognized on the disposition); (2) net income or gain for the taxable year from all passive activities; and (3) any other income or gain.

The disposition rule can be illustrated by the following example. Assume that an individual has been involved in two rental activities, and no other passive activities. Building A, which respect to which the individual has 100x of suspended losses, is sold for a gain of 50x. Building B produces net income of 25x for the year. The 100x of suspended losses for Building A first offsets the 50x gain on the sale of Building A. The remaining 50x of loss offsets the 25x of passive income from Building B and 25x of other income (e.g., salary or dividends) of the individual.

It is unclear whether a gain realized on the sale of one passive activity (net of the suspended losses on the activity) can be offset by passive losses from other activities. Since the disposition rule operates on an activity-by-activity basis, it may be that it cannot. If so, any such gain would appear to be taxable in the year of disposition. Hopefully, this matter will be clarified soon through Treasury regulations or rulings.

A disposition of the taxpayer's entire interest in one of several activities conducted by a limited partnership, like a disposition of an activity conducted in any other form, may constitute a disposition that triggers suspended losses from that activity. Thus, if a limited partnership engages in two separate activities, it is not necessary for the taxpayer to dispose of his entire interest in both activities in order to make use of suspended losses on the activity that is disposed of.

An installment sale of the taxpayer's entire interest in an activity in a fully taxable transaction triggers the allowance of suspended losses. The suspended losses are allowed in each year of the installment obligation in the ratio that the gain recognized in each year bears to the total gain on sale.

A transfer by reason of death triggers suspended losses to the extent that they exceed the amount (if any) by which the basis of the interest in the activity is "stepped up" at death. Suspended losses are eliminated to the extent of this basis increase. Any remaining losses generally will be reported on the decedent's final tax return.

With respect to tax credits that have not been used because of the loss limitation, the new law provides an election in the case of a fully taxable disposition of an interest in an activity where a basis adjustment was made as a result of placing the property in service (e.g., where a taxpayer reduces depreciable basis by the amount of rehabilitation tax credit claimed). Upon such a disposition, the taxpayer may elect to increase the basis of the credit property (by an amount no greater than the amount of the original basis reduction) to the extent that the credit has not previously been allowed by reason of the passive loss limitation. At the time of the basis adjustment election, the amount of the suspended credit that subsequently may be applied against tax liability is reduced by the amount of the basis adjustment.

This basis adjustment is illustrated by the following example. Assume that a taxpayer places in service property generating an allowable rehabilitation tax credit of 20x. As required by law, the taxpayer reduces the basis of the property by 20x. Assume further that, in the year the taxpayer sells the property, the taxpayer has not been able to use any amount of the rehabilitation tax credit due to the passive loss limitation. In the year of sale, the taxpayer may elect to increase the basis of the property by 20x. This basis increase, along with any suspended losses triggered upon sale, reduces the amount of gain to be recognized from the sale of the property.

To the extent that any loss recognized on a fully taxable disposition of a taxpayer's entire interest in a passive activity is a loss from the sale or exchange of a capital asset, such loss is limited to the amount of gains from the sale or exchange of capital assets plus $3,000 (in the case of individuals). For example, assume a taxpayer has a capital loss of $15,000 upon the disposition of a passive activity, and is also allowed to deduct $10,000 of previously suspended ordinary losses as a result of the disposition. The $10,000 of ordinary losses are allowed, but the capital loss deduction is limited to $3,000 for the year (assuming no other capital gains or losses for the year). Any capital losses not allowed upon disposition are carried forward under the capital loss carryforward rules.

Active Participation Exception

The new law provides a special and limited exception from the passive loss limit for rental real estate. Certain individuals may offset up to $25,000 of income that is not treated as passive (e.g., salary income or active business income) by using losses from rental real estate activities with respect to which the individuals "actively participate." The $25,000 loss exception applies to the rehabilitation and low-income housing tax credits in a deduction-equivalent sense, whether or not the taxpayer actively participates (e.g., a taxpayer could claim a low-income housing tax credit of up to $7,000--28 percent of $25,000--against tax attributable to salary income).

This $25,000 allowance is applied by first netting income and loss from all of the taxpayer's rental real estate activities in which he actively participates. If there is a net loss for the year from such activities, then any net passive income from other activities is applied against such net loss in determining the amount eligible for the $25,000 allowance. For example, if a taxpayer has $25,000 of losses from a rental real estate activity in which he actively participates and also actively participates in another rental real estate activity that produces $25,000 of income, resulting in no net loss from rental real estate in which he actively participates, then no amount would be allowed under the $25,000 allowance.

The $25,000 loss allowance is reduced by 50 percent of the amount by which the taxpayer's adjusted gross income for the taxable year exceeds $100,000. For example, a taxpayer with adjusted gross income of $125,000 would be entitled to a loss allowance of $12,500. A taxpayer whose adjusted gross income is $150,000 or more would not be entitled to any special loss allowance. For purposes of the special loss allowance, adjusted gross income is determined without regard to net losses from passive activities (other than losses resulting from a fully taxable disposition of an activity). Furthermore, adjusted gross income is calculated without regard to IRA contributions and taxable social security benefits.

The adjusted gross income phase-out range for the rehabilitation and low-income housing tax credits is between $200,000 and $250,000. Thus, for example, an individual with $200,000 or less of adjusted gross income could claim up to $7,000 of rehabilitation tax credits for the year without limitation.

In general, in the case of married taxpayers who file separate returns, the $25,000 loss allowance (and the adjusted gross income ranges in which the allowance is phased out) is cut in half. However, if married taxpayers who file separately live together, at any time during the taxble year, then no special loss allowance is available.

As noted above, the $25,000 loss allowance is available to certain individuals who actively participate in rental real estate activities. The standard for active participation is substantially less stringent than the standard for material participation. That is, the active participation requirement can be satisfied without regular, continuous, and substantial involvement in operations. However, to meet the active participation standard, the taxpayer must participate, for example, in the making of management decisions or arranging for others to provide services, in a significant and bona fide sense. Relevant management decisions in this context include approving new tenants, deciding on rental terms, approving capital or repair expenditures, and other similar decisions. The fact that management services are contracted out will not, by itself, cause a taxpayer to fail the active participation standard so long as the taxpayer exercises independent judgment and authority. However, mere ratification of other's judgments likely will result in the standard not being met.

A taxpayer will not be treated as an active participant in a rental real estate activity if he owns less than 10 percent of all interests in the activity. Furthermore, a limited partner cannot meet the active participation standard to the extent of his limited partnership interest. However, neither of these requirements apply in the case of rehabilitation or low-income housing tax credits, both of which may be claimed by certain individuals without regard to active participation.

The Potential for Passive Income

It is important to note that the strict definition of material participation in a business activity opens up significant potential for arranging a taxpayer's business affairs such that he or she does not materially participate in an activity that can generate substantial income for the taxpayer. For example, if a builder/developer owns a management company producing net income and if his activities with respect to the operation of the company truly do not constitute "material participation," then it appears that the income from the business will be passive and, thus, eligible to be offset by passive losses from rental real estate activities. Treasury regulations may attempt to prevent such a characterization, yet it would seem somewhat odd that the material participation standard would be made very strict for activities generating losses but not so strict for activities generating income.

Another strategy for minimizing passive losses is to assure that the minimum appropriate charge is made by an activity that generates non-passive income, such as property management, to activities that generate passive losses, such as an apartment building. Likewise, the maximum appropriate rent should be charged for office space used by income-generating activities.

Effective Date and Phase-in Rules

In general, the passive loss limitation is effective for taxable years beginning after December 31, 1986. However, a special phase-in rule applies in the case of any passive activity loss or credit for any taxable year beginning in calendar years 1987 through 1990 which is attributable to an interest acquired on or before the date of enactment (October 22, 1986). Under this phase-in rule, a percentage of pre-enactment losses is made subject to the passive loss limitation in accordance with the following table:

Taxable years beginning in:	Percentage of Losses Subject to Limitation
1987	35 percent
1988	60 percent
1989	80 percent
1990	90 percent
1991	100 percent

For example, assume that a taxpayer, who has interests in no other passive activities bought a limited partnership interest in an apartment project on October 22, 1986. Assume, further, that the taxpayer's net passive activity loss from the apartment project is $10,000 for his 1987 taxable year. The taxpayer would be able to deduct, without limitation, $6,500 of the loss. The remaining $3,500 would be subject to the passive activity loss limitation. Interests acquired after the date of enactment are fully subject to the passive loss rule.

A contractual obligation to purchase an interest in a passive activity that is binding on the date of enactment is treated as an acquisition of the interest, and, thus, qualifies for the phase-in treatment. A binding contract qualifies even if subject to contingencies, so long as the contingencies are beyond the resonable control of the taxpayer.

If investors contribute additional capital to an activity after October 22, 1986, their interests still qualify for full relief under the phase-in to the extent that their percentage ownership interests do not change as a result of the contribution. However, if a taxpayer's ownership interest increases after October 22, 1986, then, in general, the portion of his interest attributable to the increase does not qualify for phase-in relief.

In order to qualify for phase-in relief, the interest acquired by a taxpayer generally must be in an activity that has commenced by the date of enactment. A rental activity commences when the rental property has been placed in service in the activity. In the case an activity that has not commenced by the date of enactment, phase-in relief applies if the entity (or an individual owning the activity) has entered into a binding contract effective on or before August 16, 1986, to acquire the assets used to conduct the activity. Likewise, phase-in relief applies in the case of self-constructed business property where construction of the property to be used in the activity has commenced on or before August 16, 1986.

If a taxpayer owns both pre-enactment and post-enactment interests in passive activities, it is necessary to determine the amount of passive loss that would be disallowed absent the phase-in. The phase-in relief applies to the lesser of the taxpayer's total passive loss, or the passive loss taking into account only pre-enactment interests. For example, if a taxpayer has $10,000 of passive loss relating to pre-enactment interests that would be disallowed in absence of the phase-in, and has $6,000 of net passive income from post-enactment interests, resulting in a total passive loss of $4,000, then the phase-in relief applies to the lesser of $10,000 or $4,000 (i.e., $4,000). This implies that any injection of passive income intended to utilize passive losses will be diluted by the phase-in rules.

Any passive loss that is disallowed for a taxable year during the phase-in period and carried forward is allowable in a subsequent year only to the extent that there is net passive income in the subsequent year (or there is a fully taxable disposition of the activity). The phase-in allowance does not apply to it. The applicable phase-in percentage for any transition year applies to the passive loss net of any portion of such loss that may be allowed against non-passive income under the $25,000 loss allowance for active participants. In other words, the $25,000 exception is applied to the aggregate net passive losses before phase-in and not to the remaining unutilized losses after the phase-in calulation. Specific transition relief is provided for certain investments in low-income housing. In general, losses from certain investments made after 1983 are excepted from the passive activity loss limitation for a period of up to seven years from the date of the taxpayer's original investment. This "grandfather" exception is discussed more fully in the Appendix.

IRS Regulations

The Treasury Department has been granted broad regulatory authority with regard to the passive activity loss limitation. Congress has instructed the Treasury to prescribe such regulations as may be necessary or appropriate in regard to the passive loss limitation, including regulations:

* Which specify what constitutes an activity, material participation, or active participation;

* Which provide that certain types of gross income will not be taken into account in determining income or loss from any activity;

* Requiring net income or gain from a limited partnership or other passive activity to be treated as not from a passive activity;

* Which provide for the determination of the allocation of interest expense; and

* Which deal with changes in marital status and changes between joint returns and separate returns.

THE INVESTMENT INTEREST LIMITATION

Prior law provided that, in the case of a noncorporate taxpayer (e.g., an individual), deductions for interest on debt incurred or continued to purchase or carry property held for investment were generally limited to $10,000 per year, plus the taxpayer's net investment income and certain deductible expenditures in excess of rental income from net lease property. Investment interest that exceeded this limitation was subject to an unlimited carryover and could be deducted in future years.

The new law limits the deduction for investment interest to only the amount of investment income i.e., the $10,000 allowance no longer is permitted. Interest that is disallowed in any taxable year is carried forward and treated as investment interest in the succeeding taxable year. Interest that is carried forward to subsequent years is allowed as a deduction in such years only to the extent of the taxpayer's net investment income.

For purposes of this limitation, investment interest includes the following types of interest:

* Interest paid or accrued on indebtedness incurred or continued to purchase or carry property held for investment;

* Interest expense properly allocable to portfolio income under the passive activity loss limitation;

* Interest expense properly allocable to an activity involving a trade or business in which the taxpayer does not materially participate, if that activity is not treated as a passive activity under the passive loss limitation, and

* Interest expense incurred or continued to purchase or carry an interest in a passive activity, to the extent attributable to portfolio income.

Investment interest does not include any of the following types of interest:

* Interest that is taken into account in determining the taxpayer's income or loss from a passive activity;

* Interest properly allocable to a rental real estate activity in which the taxpayer actively participates;

* Interest related to the conduct of a trade or business in which the taxpayer materially participates; and

* Qualified residence interest.

Investment income, for purposes of this limitation, includes gross income from property held for investment (e.g., stock dividends), gain attributable to the disposition of property held for investment, and amounts treated as gross portfolio income under the passive loss rule. It does not include income from a rental real estate activity in which the taxpayer actively participates. Net investment income is investment income net of investment expenses (i.e., deductible expenses directly connected with the production of investment income). Investment expenses are those allowed after application of the rule limiting deductions for miscellaneous expenses to those exceeding two percent of the taxpayer's adjusted gross income. In computing the amount of expenses that exceed this floor, investment expenses are "stacked" on top of other miscellaneous non-investment expenses.

The new law also disallows deductions for personal interest, including interest on tax deficiencies. For this purpose, personal interest generally is any interest other than interest incurred or continued in connection with the conduct of a trade or business, investment interest, interest taken into account in computing income or loss from passive activities, interest payable on deferred estate taxes, or qualified residence interest.

Effective Dates

The investment interest limitation is phased in, effective for taxable years beginning after December 31, 1986. Interest that was not disallowed under prior law (e.g., consumer interest or the first $10,000 of investment interest), but which is disallowed under the new law, becomes subject to disallowance of 35 percent in taxable years beginning in 1987, 60 percent in taxable years beginning in 1988, 80 percent in taxable years beginning in 1989, 90 percent in taxable years beginning in 1990, and 100 percent in taxable years beginning after 1990.

The amount of investment interest disallowed during the phase-in period is the excess over the amount of the prior law $10,000 allowance plus the applicable portion of investment interest expense that would be disallowed without taking into account the prior law allowance. For example, if an individual has $15,000 of investment interest expense in excess of investment income in 1987, 35 percent of the amount that does not exceed $10,000 (or $3,500) plus all of the amount in excess of $10,000 (or $5,000) would be disallowed. Thus, for 1987, $8,500 would be disallowed and $6,500 would be allowed.

For purposes of the investment interest limitation, for taxable years beginning on or after January 1, 1987 and before January 1, 1991, net investment income is reduced by the amount of losses from passive activities that is allowed as a deduction under the phase-in of the passive loss rule (other than net losses from rental real estate in which the taxpayer actively participates). That is, a passive activity loss that is allowed under the passive loss phase-in rule reduces the taxpayer's net investment income under the investment interest limitation.

Finally, investment interest that is disallowed under the investment interest limitation during the phase-in period is only allowed as a deduction in a subsequent year to the extent the taxpayer has net investment income in excess of investment interest in the subsequent year.

THE AT-RISK RULES

Under prior law, there was an at-risk limitation on losses from business and income-producing activities other than real estate. That is, in order to deduct losses from those activities, a taxpayer had to be at risk for at least that amount in the activities. In general, the amount that a taxpayer has at risk in an activity is the sum of the following amounts:

* The taxpayer's cash contributions to the activity;

* The adjusted basis of property other than cash contributed to the activity; and

* Amounts borrowed for use in the activity with respect to which the taxpayer has personal liability or has pledged property not used in the activity.

The new law generally extends the at-risk rules to the activity of holding real property. However, an exception is provided for third-party nonrecourse debt borrowed from an unrelated commercial lender. Furthermore, related-party nonrecourse financing from a commercial lender qualifies for exception from the at-risk rules, in the case of real estate, if the terms of the loan are commercially reasonable and on substantially the same terms as loans involving unrelated persons. In general, the terms of nonrecourse financing will be commercially reasonable if the financing is a written unconditional promise to pay on demand, or on a specified date or dates, a sum or sums certain in money, and the interest rate is a reasonable market rate of interest.

The new at-risk rules should not prove to be generally troublesome in most cases. Even real estate joint ventures will be allowed to obtain amounts at risk for financing from an otherwise qualified lender that has an interest in the venture if the terms of the loan are commercially reasonable and substantially similar to loans made to unrelated parties. The major drawback, however, of the new rules will be that seller financing will not be treated as qualified nonrecourse financing exempt from the at-risk rules. This may be particularly troublesome for transactions involving foreclosed property or federally-assisted low-income housing projects.

The revision of the at-risk rules is effective for property placed in service after December 31, 1986, and for losses attributable to an interest in a partnership, subchapter S corporation, or other pass-through entity that is acquired after December 31, 1986.

INDIVIDUAL MINIMUM TAX

The minimum tax takes on new importance because of significant base broadening under the new law and due to the reduced disparity between the minimum tax rate and the top regular tax rate. Currently the minimum tax rate is 20 percent compared to a top regular tax rate of 50 percent. In 1988, when the rate cuts are fully phased in the top regular tax rate will be 28 percent compared to a minimum tax rate of 21 percent.

Currently, individuals are subject to an alternative minimum tax, which applies to a broader income base (regular taxable income plus tax preferences) and at a lower rate than the regular tax. This minimum tax is payable to the extent that it exceeds regular tax liability.

As already noted, the rate is increased to 21 percent and the base is broadened substantially. As under prior law, alternative minimum taxable income is reduced by an exemption amount of $40,000 for joint returns, $30,000 for singles, and $20,000 for married taxpayers filing separately. However, this exemption amount will be reduced by 25 cents for each $1 by which alternative minimum taxable income exceeds $150,000 ($112,500 for single returns and $75,000 for marrieds filing separately). This phase-out of the exemption amount will tend to make more taxpayers subject to the minimum tax. However, the elimination of the long-term capital gain exclusion amount as a minimum tax preference item may end up more than offsetting the phase-out and result in fewer individuals paying the minimum tax.

Under the new law, tax preferences for purposes of the minimum tax will include the following items:

* **Accelerated depreciation on real property.** Present law applies to property placed in service by the end of 1986 and to property that is grandfathered under the depreciation rules. For real property placed in service after 1986, the preference is the excess of regular tax depreciation over the amount of depreciation under the alternative depreciation system. For residential buildings, this is the difference between 27 1/2 year straight-line depreciation and 40 year straight-line depreciation. For commercial buildings, this is the difference between 31 1/2 year straight-line depreciation and 40 year straight-line depreciation. However, there is no depreciation preference if the alternative depreciation system is elected for regular tax purposes (i.e., 40 year straight-line depreciation for buildings).

* **Accelerated depreciation on personal property.** For personal property placed in service after 1986, the preference is the excess of regular tax depreciation over alternative depreciation.

* **Expensing of intangible drilling costs.** The excess of expensing over 10-year amortization or cost depletion, to the extent in excess of 65 percent of net oil and gas income, is a preference.

* **60-month amortization on certified pollution control facilites.** The excess over depreciation allowed under the alternative depreciation system is a preference.

* **Expensing of mining exploration and development costs.** The excess of expensing over 10-year amortization is a preference.

* **Percentage depletion.** The excess over the adjusted basis of the depletable property is a preference.

* **Net capital gains.** Since the net capital gain deduction has been repealed, net capital gains are included fully in both minimum and regular taxable income.

* **Incentive stock options.** The excess of the fair market value of stock over the exercise price is a preference.

* **Tax-exempt interest.** Tax-exempt interest on newly-issued private activity bonds (e.g., mortgage revenue bonds and multifamily industrial development bonds) other than qualified tax-exempt organization bonds is treated as a preference. In general, treatment as a preference applies to bonds issued on or after August 8, 1986.

* **Completed contract and other methods of accounting for long-term contracts.** Use of the completed contract or another method of accounting for long-term contracts that permits deferral of income during the contract period is treated as a preference, by requiring use of the percentage of completion method for minimum tax purposes on post March 1, 1986 long-term contracts.

* **Installment method of accounting.** Use of the installment method of accounting by dealers in real or personal property, or with respect to sales of trade or business or rental property where the purchase price exceeds $150,000, is denied for minimum tax purposes, i.e., all deferred gain is included in the minimum tax base. However, sellers of unimproved residential lots and timeshares may elect to pay interest on the deferral of income. The denial of installment sales treatment applies to sales on or after March 1, 1986.

* **Net loss from passive trade or business activities.** The passive loss rules of the regular tax apply for purposes of the minimum tax. Unlike the regular tax, however, no phase-in relief is provided. Thus, excess passive activity losses arising after December 31, 1986, are denied in full for purposes of the minimum tax.

* **Losses from passive farming activities.** Excess passive farm losses are treated as a preference.

* **Charitable contributions of appreciated property.** In the case of charitable contributions of appreciated property, the amount of untaxed appreciation allowed as a regular tax deduction is treated as a preference. For example, assume a taxpayer bought a painting for $1,000 and gives it to a charitable organization when its fair market value is $10,000. For regular tax purposes, he claims a $10,000 charitable contribution deduction. For purposes of the minimum tax $9,000 would be treated as a preference item.

The itemized deductions that are allowed for minimum tax purposes, are those for casualty and theft losses, gambling losses to the extent of winnings, charitable deductions, medical deductions to the extent in excess of 10 percent of adjusted gross income, interest expenses (i.e., housing interest and investment interest to the extent of investment income), and certain estate taxes. Miscellaneous deductions and itemized deductions for state and local taxes are not allowed. Furthermore, the new investment interest limitation is not phased in for minimum tax purposes.

Individuals will be allowed a credit against their regular tax liabilities in future years, based upon a portion of alternative minimum tax paid in prior years after 1986. This credit will be available to the extent of prior year deferral preferences (e.g., depreciation). It will not be available to the extent that prior year minimum tax liability was attributable to excess percentage depletion, tax-exempt interest, contributions of appreciated property, or non-minimum tax itemized deductions.

Even though individuals may have no current minimum tax liability, they will be well advised to keep track of tax preference items on an annual basis in order to make the adjustments required in calculating the minimum tax in future years.

The new minimum tax structure applies for taxable years beginning after December 31, 1986.

THE CORPORATE MINIMUM TAX

Under prior law, corporations paid an "add-on" minimum tax. This tax was equal to 15 percent of tax preferences minus regular tax paid.

The new law provides for a corporate alternative minimum tax, at a rate of 20 percent, which is similar in structure to the individual minimum tax. This minimum tax is payable to the extent that it exceeds regular tax liabilities. In addition, the new law requires corporations to make estimated tax payments of minimum tax liability, as well as regular tax liabilities.

With minor variations, items of tax preference for purposes of the corporate minimum tax are similar to items of tax preference for purposes of the individual minimum tax. However, there is no passive loss preference for corporations since corporations generally are not subject to the passive loss restrictions.

A new tax preference for corporations that is of major importance is business untaxed reported profits. For the years 1987-1989, this preference will consist of one-half of the amount by which the adjusted net book income of a corporation exceeds the alternative minimum taxable income of the corporation. After 1989, earnings and profits will replace book income. Corporations that compute their net income for all financial statement purposes exclusively in accordance with tax accounting rules will not have this book/tax preference. Book/tax differences generally arise because (1) the timing of the recognition of items of income, expense, loss, or deduction is different for book and tax purposes, or (2) for either book or tax purposes, an item of income is exempt, excluded, or not recognized, or an item of expense or loss is not allowable, deductible, or recognized.

A common example of when this book/tax preference may arise is with respect to tax-exempt municipal bond interest. If such interest is reported for financial statement purposes, it will be treated as a preference item.

The revisions to the corporate minimum tax are effective for taxable years beginning after December 31, 1986.

Chapter 4

NEW APPROACHES TO RENTAL FINANCE

Steven S. Heyman
Partner
Colton and Boykin
Washington, D.C.

THE FINANCING ENVIRONMENT AND TAX REFORM

The construction of multifamily residential apartment projects is largely dependent upon a builder/developer securing enough equity capital to satisfy a conventional lender's equity requirements. Prior to the Tax Reform Act of 1986 a major, if not the largest, equity capital source for multifamily construction was the sale of limited partnership interests through a syndication, with the developer acting as a general partner. The syndication of real estate offered investors cash flow, appreciation and substantial tax benefits. However, the tax benefits were often the major draw, sometimes being in excess of 250 percent of an investor's required cash contributions during a four to six year pay-in period. Such large tax benefits attracted capital from investors who were less concerned with economic return, as they could partially offset their wage, dividend, and interest income. High-income taxpayers and moderate-income taxpayers suffering "bracket creep" increasingly funneled available investment dollars into real estate in an effort to reduce tax liability.

The Act changes a number of provisions which provided the underpinning for the participation of individuals in limited partnerships, including accelerated depreciation, rapid amortization of construction period interest and taxes, and the capital gains exclusion of a portion of recaptured depreciation at time of sale. Of equal significance, the Act attacks the concept of using tax losses on rental real estate to shelter income from other activities. In general, the ability of investors in "passive activities" to offset tax losses against wages and portfolio income (e.g., interest and dividends) is phased out for existing investments and eliminated for new investments. Passive activities are those trade or business activities in which the taxpayer does not materially participate (e.g.,limited partnership interests), and all rental activities. (Chapter 3 examines the many important details of how this limitation will work, and Chapter 2 discusses the Act's impacts on rental markets in general.)

In light of the passive loss restrictions and other changes under the Act which will adversely affect real estate, investors will only put their capital at risk in real estate if the investment provides a cash-on-cash return which generates a yield premium commensurate with the risk and comparative illiquidity of a real estate investment. This is generally not the case at current rent levels in most markets. Studies indicate that it will take several years (depending, of course, upon particular market conditions) for rentals on multifamily projects to reflect the continuing slowdown in new construction. In housing markets which have been the subject of overbuilding, the rental adjustment period could be longer. The length of the recovery period will be generally based upon simple supply-demand economics. However, the point to be made is that under the Act, rental income and property appreciation will be the building blocks of an investor's yield.

MULTIFAMILY FINANCING AFTER TAX REFORM

The key question now is what investment entities and structures will be most suitable for multifamily financing, both during and after the transition to the "post tax-shelter" world. The search for new approaches actually began several months ago, when it became apparent that Congress was likely to enact major tax changes. That search has resulted in a shift towards new construction which uses creative financing techniques and taps new investor markets. Several of the most promising approaches now being used are discussed below.

100 Percent Financing Including Lender Participation

Participating loans are not new. In a typical participating loan, the lender charges a below-market interest rate on a loan and "strips" a piece of the borrower's appreciation at the earlier of the maturity of the loan or the sale of the project. There may also be a participation in cash flow. In effect, the lender foregoes an equity capital infusion adequate to satisfy its usual loan-to-value requirement and assumes an economic position similar to that of a limited partner in a syndication. While the participation is intended to compensate the lender for its assumption of economic risk, participating in either cash flow or appreciation likely leads the lender to establish very conservative underwriting criteria. The below-market interest rate reduces the developer's interest cost over the life of the project, thereby reducing the chance that the developer or other owners will experience losses which must be suspended under the passive loss rules.

Certain tax and legal issues need to be addressed in structuring a participation because the debt instrument must not be subject to recharacterization as equity. If properly structured, a participating loan should retain its legal status as debt, as opposed to equity. The advantage of 100 percent financing is clear: the developer does not have to put substantial equity dollars of its own at risk, although it must provide completion and property performance guarantees and/or letters of credit. In fact, the developer's present value cost is less than the "piece of the deal" it must give up to the equity capital investors in a syndication. Besides earning substantial construction and development fees, the developer can independently control the project and its disposition (subject to certain limited restrictions typically imposed by the participating lender), while earning an attractive cash-on-cash return attributable to the below market interest charge. In addition, the developer need not spend time and resources finding large equity investors with sufficient passive income to be able to utilize any losses thrown off by the project.

Lenders (including, in particular, insurance companies and pension funds) are demonstrating an increasing willingness to underwrite participating loans. This trend should continue if interest rates remain relatively low. Therefore, participating loans offer builder/developers an excellent opportunity to deliver their product to market at a minimal direct investment cost.

Changing the Mix of Debt to Equity

Builder/developers also might consider reducing a project's debt-to-equity ratio. Cash flow from operations--that would otherwise be used to service debt in a more traditional, highly leveraged deal--can then be distributed to the partners contributing the substantial equity capital. The reduction in debt service allows for a competitive investor yield and the minimization of tax losses that might otherwise be suspended. As with a participating loan, the builder/developer typically guarantees equity investors both construction completion and project performance. Although the substantial equity requirements dilute the developer's percentage interest in the deal, substantial fees and a piece of the deal are some compensation.

The equity investor market shows signs of responding positively to one-property transactions involving small projected losses, positive cash flow (partially or fully sheltered) and an opportunity for appreciation. This type of structure has already achieved market appeal for existing properties, but is relatively untested in new construction. A number of recent offerings which have raised funds for multifamily apartment acquisitions are based on the premise that 30 to 50 percent of a project's cost should be paid from equity (as opposed to debt) sources. Existing properties with strong lease histories can immediately produce income, given the proper debt/equity mix and if the purchase price is low enough.

Also, if the percentage of debt is low enough, investors are likely to have some taxable income, an appealing feature to investors whose prior real estate investments are still generating passive losses; the income will enable those investors to currently deduct losses rather than carry them forward. Thus, individual investors should constitute a significant equity source for lower-debt deals.

Use of Zero Coupon Bonds

Zero coupon bonds are debt instruments which do not provide for any current payments of principal or interest. Interest is accrued, added to principal and compounded, with all principal and interest becoming due at maturity of the obligation. The risk to investors purchasing zero coupon bonds is that proceeds from the eventual sale of the underlying property will not be sufficient to pay off the bonds. As a result, zero coupon bonds often require a form of credit enhancement to assure full payment of principal and interest to bondholders at maturity. Furthermore, the sale proceeds also must provide a return to the developer. By financing with zeros, the developer can retain more project cash flow. Pension funds and insurance companies have already been a receptive market for zero coupon bonds, partially because such investments satisfy actuarial needs. Moreover, low interest rates have made them highly competitive.

Zero coupon bonds, secured by a first mortgage on the project, have a low risk position because they typically provide less than 50 percent of the total project cost. Nevertheless, conservative pricing is required to successfully market a zero coupon bond. The accreted value of the bonds at maturity (that is, including the accrued interest which is to be added to principal and compounded) should not be greater than 70 to 80 percent of the project's appraised value at the time of construction completion. The builder/developer must use conventional or participating second mortgage debt or investor equity to finance the remainder of the construction cost. If a zero coupon bond is coupled with a conventional second mortgage offering, the developer will probably be required to provide some equity. However, if a zero coupon is coupled with a participating second mortgage, a deal can probably be structured which will provide 100 percent financing. The builder/developer will typically be required to provide construction completion and property performance guarantees.

Investor risk depends on the financing mix. The investors in the second mortgage offering have a greater risk position (typical of a second mortgage). The obligation of paying the accreting interest component of the zero coupon bond from sale proceeds may impinge on the expected interest return for investors in a participating second mortgage offering. However, this risk is offset by the yield premium such investors should enjoy from the participation. The internal rate of return on this type of second mortgage can exceed Treasuries of comparable maturity by 200 to 250 percent. As is the case in any creative construction loan financing, the investor's risk is greatest during the construction period. Therefore, whether a public offering or private placement is used to provide the debt financing, market response depends on builder reputation.

Investors purchasing a zero coupon bond must report income attributable to the accrued interest component even though no cash payment is made. This creates "phantom income" for the investor, that is, a tax liability without an equivalent cash payment to the taxpayer. Accordingly, tax-exempt entities are the preferred investor source for this type of instrument.

It may be most desirable to combine the above financing techniques. For example, a financing package could be negotiated to provide 100 percent financing, including a dual debt offering of taxable bonds secured by a first mortgage and a participating second mortgage offering.

Master Limited Partnerships

Master limited partnerships ("MLPs") are a comparatively new form of ownership for real estate, especially for existing properties.* MLPs are limited partnerships in which the partnership interests are traded on a national stock exchange. Investor interest in MLPs is high because, in contrast to most limited partnerships and other real estate investments, the ownership shares are liquid, allowing investors who need cash or currently cannot use the tax losses to sell their shares. Despite this liquidity, the investors still avoid double taxation: MLP income is taxed only at the

---

MLPs are also being used for the holding of active trades or businesses, including home building, instead of the usual corporate form. The current focus on MLPs relates to their desirability for holding assets, such as real estate or oil and gas. Between now and the end of the year, one commentator projects that up to $2 billion of non-oil-and-gas MLPs will come to market as initial public offerings. However, the Treasury Department has expressed concern about lost revenues resulting from the structuring of active businesses as MLPs rather than corporations, and it is possible that legislation may be enacted in the future which will adversely affect the current tax status of MLPs.

investor level. Essentially, MLPs are public partnership offerings that are large scale enough to also offer liquidity.

Some MLPs use zero coupon financing to enhance current cash flow and are targeted for real estate acquisitions (although they may become a viable instrument in new construction). Moreover, in the past several years, several oil and gas sponsors have "rolled up" their small private partnerships into MLPs. In addition, older partnerships generating significant income can be rolled up with recent ones showing losses. To exchange an interest in a private partnership for an interest in an MLP, all properties to be rolled up must be appraised. Units in the old partnerships are exchanged for interests in the new MLP, based on these valuations. In addition, higher cash distributions can be promised to investors if loan balances are reduced through refinancing as part of the roll-up.

GENERAL OBSERVATIONS

Pension funds (both public and private), insurance companies (which are particularly receptive to participations), and institutional investors are the preferred sources of debt financing that developers should look to in financing multifamily construction after the Act. In 1984, for example, insurers invested 10 percent of all new mortgage loans they made in multifamily apartments. That figure increased to 15 percent last year and should continue to rise. Moreover, the willingness of the secondary mortgage market to accept the securitization of multifamily mortgage loans has made such financing more palatable to insurers and institutional investors. Although the secondary mortgage market has been reluctant to underwrite and market a security backed by a single apartment building because of the lack of diversification and geographic dispersal of such an issue, there is growing interest in the issuance of securities collaterized by a pool of apartment mortgages. Standard and Poor's recently issued guidelines for the rating of such securitized mortgages.

Pension funds, insurance companies and institutional investors also are expected to become more significant investors in multifamily real estate after tax reform, particularly if interest rates remain low or continue to decline. These investment groups are not concerned about the loss of tax benefits and are attracted by the high current yields and the protection against inflation that real estate can offer. However, they have historically had a clear preference for debt over equity, in part because of their familiarity with that form of investment (as opposed to equity) and in part because of certain legal constraints. For example, private pension funds are subject to strict fiduciary standards which make their participation in equity offerings difficult; moreover, proposed regulatory restrictions scheduled to apply as of January 1, 1987 will expand the definition of "plan assets," as a result of which their participation in equity offerings will be severely limited. Lastly, the adverse tax consequences to tax-exempt entities of an equity investment, such as unrelated business taxable income, effectively restrict their participation in real estate finance to investment in debt instruments.

Another shift in the market which was already taking place is the expanding presence of foreign equity investors. The decline of the dollar and the high yields on U.S. real estate relative to foreign properties are drawing foreign interest. The decline in tax advantages will further bolster the competitiveness of foreign investors relative to domestic investors.

These innovations in financing offer developers an opportunity to bring their product to market. Although the seductive internal rates of return available before tax reform will not be restored by any novel financing vehicle, the opportunity (of a debt or equity investor) to earn a 13 to 16 percent internal rate of return is real, achievable in many areas, and very competitive against other investments. From an investor's point of view, the issue is whether the increased yield premium is commensurate with the real or perceived additional risks of real estate over other investments. Investors are likely to be more selective than ever in evaluating real estate opportunities. Similarly, developers will be forced to be more selective in locating properties that will generate a significant economic return. This could lead to a split market in multifamily similar to that in commercial real estate, where top quality space is financed by institutional sources and other space requires higher yields to attract funds from individual investors.

Chapter 5

THE NEW RULES FOR HOUSING FINANCE

David L. Ledford
Director of Market Analysis for Mortgage Finance
National Association of Home Builders

The Tax Act should have several effects on the way in which mortgage funds flow from investors and lenders to home buyers. Tougher restrictions on tax-exempt housing bonds, which provide mortgage money for first-time home buyers and financing for low-income rental housing, will diminish the role of state and local housing finance agencies in the mortgage marketplace. Builder involvement in home lending will also decline, curbed by the loss of their ability to defer taxes by issuing mortgage-backed "builder" bonds. Revised tax rules seem likely to encourage a reduction in mortgage holdings of thrift institutions. Finally, the secondary market in mortgage loans will undergo a change as a result of a new vehicle for issuing mortgage securities with a choice of maturities.

CHANGES IN TAX-EXEMPT FINANCING

The Tax Act contains major changes in the areas of tax-exempt financing. The legislation reclassifies the current tax-exempt market for general obligation and revenue bonds into "public-use" and "private-use" bonds. The bill restricts the range of private uses that are eligible for tax-exempt funding and reduces the annual volume of bonds that may be issued for the remaining permitted uses. In addition, several other provisions of the bill affect investors in tax-exempt securities, and these measures may result in somewhat higher relative borrowing costs on private-use tax-exempt issues. In the area of housing, there is also a general tightening of eligibility requirements for homeowners and renters benefitting from tax-exempt bond programs.

Limitation on Bond Volume

The broadest provision affecting the availability of tax-exempt funds for housing uses is the private-activity bond volume limitation. Both single family mortgage revenue bonds (MBRs) and industrial development bonds for multifamily projects (IDBs) retain their tax-exempt status, but MBRs and IDBs are placed under a unified annual volume cap that applies to most permitted private-use tax-exempt securites. MRBs were formerly subject to a separate volume limitation that was based on each state's average mortgage activity, while rental housing IDBs faced no volume limitations. Under the Act, state annual volume ceilings for private-purpose tax-exempt bond issues are set at the greater of $75 per capita or $250 million until 1988. From 1988 on, the limit will be the greater of $50 per capita or $150 million. The exclusion of some bonds from the volume cap and elimination of tax-exempt status for a number of private uses thins out the ranks of competitors for state annual bond allocations, but competition for private-use bond authority should be heated, particularly in states that are large issuers relative to population.

To help gauge this competition, Exhibit 5.1 lists private-purpose bond volume in 1984 and 1985, grouped according to new tax law treatment. Tax-exempt housing bonds and the remaining permitted private use issues initially will be competing for a total national bond allocation of roughly $22 billion. This limit accommodates less than 40 percent of the 1985 volume of issues that are now under the private activity cap. The ceiling covers a bit more than half of capped private activity bonds issued in 1984, a year where tax-exempt bond activity was less influenced by anticipated tax law changes.

In the near term, the volume cap may prove to be less restrictive than suggested by the 1984 and 1985 activity figures. First, the cap for the current year only applies to bonds issued after August 15, 1986, placing only four and-one-half months of activity under the full-year limit. Second, bond authority may be carried forward and therefore whatever is not used in 1986 will be available in 1987. Third, small issue IDBs (except those for manufacturing facilities) will no longer qualify for tax-exempt status after 1986. Removing these small issue bonds from the 1984 totals lifts the cap's coverage to 84 percent of other bond issues.

Exhibit 5.1
Private Activity Bonds

Bonds Under the Cap	New Issues ($ millions) 1984	1985
Single Family Housing (MRBs, Sunset 12/31/88)	12,758	12,161
Multifamily Housing	5,379	23,577
Student Loans	1,370	2,902
Privately-owned Solid Waste Disposal*	N.A.	N.A.
Water Furnishing Facilities	136	70
Mass Transportation Facilities	7	11
District Heating and Cooling	103	13
Local Electric and Gas	419	880
Hazardous Waste	N.A.	N.A.
Redevelopment Bonds	N.A.	N.A.
Small-issue IDBs (Sunset 12/31/86**)	17,302	16,094
	37,474	55,708

Bonds Excluded from Cap		
Qualified 501(c)(3) Bonds	9,119	26,044
Airports, Docks, and Wharves	3,713	3,452
Publicly-owned Solid Waste Disposal*	6,644	5,086
Veterans' Mortgage Bonds	1,992	965
	21,468	35,547

Bonds Losing Tax-Exempt Status	New Issues ($ millions) 1984	1985
Pollution Control	7,584	5,397
Sports and Convention Facilities	573	508
Parking Facilities	N.A.	N.A.
Hydroelectric Generating Facilities	101	45
Industrial Parks	224	130
	8,482	6,080
Total Private Activity Bonds	67,424	97,335

*Information on publicly and privately owned portions not available. Total issues were attributed to publicly-owned category.
**Except for manufacturing facilities, where authority expires 12/31/89.

Sources: Bond data were compiled by the Department of Treasury, Office of Tax Analysis, from activity reported to the IRS and the Bond Buyer, except 1984 MRB data which were compiled by the U.S. Department of Housing and Urban Development.

EXHIBIT 5.2

NEW VOLUME LIMITS ON TAX-EXEMPT PRIVATE ACTIVITY BONDS

STATE	UNIFIED VOLUME CAP (1) (Millions)	TOTAL PRIVATE ACTIVITY BONDS (2) TOTAL 1984 ISSUES (Millions)	CAP AS A % OF ISSUES	HOUSING BONDS TOTAL 1984 ISSUES (Millions)	CAP AS A % OF ISSUES	MRB 1984 ISSUES (Millions)	IDB 1984 ISSUES (Millions)
ALABAMA	$302	$560	54%	$198	152%	$198	$0
ALASKA	$250	$310	81%	$202	124%	$200	$2
ARIZONA	$250	$529	47%	$186	134%	$105	$81
ARKANSAS	$250	$235	106%	$124	202%	$107	$17
CALIFORNIA	$1,977	$3,908	51%	$3,173	62%	$2,193	$980
COLORADO	$250	$589	42%	$358	70%	$241	$117
CONNECTICUT	$250	$487	51%	$271	92%	$200	$71
DELAWARE	$250	$227	110%	$82	305%	$75	$7
FLORIDA	$852	$1,981	43%	$1,092	78%	$597	$495
GEORGIA	$448	$1,195	38%	$427	105%	$186	$241
HAWAII	$250	$111	225%	$100	250%	$100	$0
IDAHO	$250	$111	225%	$56	446%	$56	$0
ILLINOIS	$865	$1,441	60%	$550	157%	$432	$118
INDIANA	$412	$604	68%	$232	178%	$200	$32
IOWA	$250	$451	55%	$240	104%	$200	$40
KANSAS	$250	$427	59%	$240	104%	$201	$39
KENTUCKY	$279	$471	59%	$204	137%	$200	$4
LOUISIANA	$336	$914	37%	$305	110%	$200	$105
MAINE	$250	$165	152%	$105	238%	$91	$14
MARYLAND	$329	$1,198	27%	$657	50%	$256	$401
MASSACHUSETTS	$437	$893	49%	$263	166%	$237	$26
MICHIGAN	$682	$966	71%	$211	323%	$145	$66
MINNESOTA	$314	$1,097	29%	$403	78%	$280	$123
MISSISSIPPI	$250	$332	75%	$220	114%	$200	$20
MISSOURI	$377	$844	45%	$451	84%	$211	$240
MONTANA	$250	$208	120%	$75	333%	$75	$0
NEBRASKA	$250	$346	72%	$236	106%	$180	$56
NEVADA	$250	$343	73%	$263	95%	$200	$63
NEW HAMPSHIRE	$250	$178	140%	$72	347%	$50	$22
NEW JERSEY	$567	$1,327	43%	$362	157%	$332	$30
NEW MEXICO	$250	$186	134%	$126	198%	$106	$20
NEW YORK	$1,334	$2,026	66%	$758	176%	$445	$313
NORTH CAROLINA	$469	$563	83%	$183	256%	$110	$73
NORTH DAKOTA	$250	$224	112%	$76	329%	$73	$3
OHIO	$806	$1,067	76%	$399	202%	$335	$64
OKLAHOMA	$250	$432	58%	$312	80%	$200	$112
OREGON	$250	$109	229%	$0	NA	$0	$0
PENNSYLVANIA	$889	$2,055	43%	$346	257%	$293	$53
RHODE ISLAND	$400	$312	128%	$233	172%	$200	$33
SOUTH CAROLINA	$251	$429	59%	$116	216%	$80	$36
SOUTH DAKOTA	$250	$292	86%	$200	125%	$200	$0
TENNESSEE	$357	$1,149	31%	$422	85%	$200	$222
TEXAS	$1,228	$2,302	53%	$1,482	83%	$1,015	$467
UTAH	$250	$451	55%	$250	100%	$198	$52
VERMONT	$250	$124	202%	$48	521%	$48	$0
VIRGINIA	$428	$1,824	23%	$698	61%	$366	$332
WASHINGTON	$331	$456	73%	$302	109%	$175	$127
WEST VIRGINIA	$250	$317	79%	$227	110%	$201	$26
WISCONSIN	$358	$543	66%	$201	178%	$191	$10
WYOMING	$250	$119	210%	$74	338%	$74	$0
OTHERS (GU,PR,DC,VI)	$607	$371	164%	$326	186%	$300	$26
TOTAL	$21,886	$37,799	58%	$18,137	121%	$12,758	$5,379

NOTES: (1) State volume limitation = the greater of $75 per resident or $250 million. State caps are based on Census Bureau provisional population estimates for July 1, 1985.
(2) Qualified 501(c)(3) bonds, bonds for airports and docks, bonds for publicly owned solid waste disposal facilities, and Veterans' mortgage bonds are not under the unified cap and have been excluded from the totals. Tax-exempt financing is no longer available for pollution control and sports and convention facilities, and these issues also have been excluded from the totals.

SOURCES: Bond data compiled by the Department of Treasury, Office of Tax Analysis from activity reported to the IRS and the Bond Buyer, except MRB data which were compiled by the U.S. Department of Housing and Urban Development.

In 1988, the drop in the per-capita allotment will produce a national private activity ceiling of approximately $14 billion. That reduced level once again covers only about half of 1984 activity, even with the exclusion of small issue IDBs. It must be recognized that, in a number of states, issues of tax-exempt private activity bonds face sharp curtailment, even at the higher initial ceiling. For housing issuers, the sharpest reduction will occur in California, Colorado, Florida, Maryland, Minnesota, and Virginia. For each of these states, the initial volume limitation for all covered bonds is less than 80 percent of even just the tax-exempt housing bonds issued in 1984 (see Exhibit 5.2).

Specific Housing Bond Provisions

In additon to the limits on private activity bond volume, the new law contains a number of provisions that place new or tighter restrictions on tax-exempt housing bond programs.

Mortgage Revenue Bonds:

An Income Cap

* A federal income limitation on persons receiving MRB loans is imposed for the first time. In most areas, the limitation is 115 percent of the higher of area or state median income. In targeted (economically depressed) areas, one-third of loans may be provided to borrowers without regard to income limits, with the balance of loans limited to borrowers with incomes not exceeding 140 percent of the higher of area or state median income.

Lower Price Limits

* The purchase price of bond-financed residences may not exceed 90 percent (110 percent in targeted areas) of the average area purchase price, down from the previous limit of 110 percent (120 percent in targeted areas).

First-Time Buyers

* The portion of MRB proceeds that must be used for loans to first-time home buyers increases to 95 percent from 90 percent. As was the case previously, there are no first-time home buyer requirements for targeted areas in a state.

New Sunset

* The sunset date for MRBs is extended one year to December 31, 1988.

Mortgage Credit Certificates: *

* Authority to issue mortgage credit certificates (MCCs) is retained under the new tax law.

* MCC targeting requirements are tightened to conform with MRB rules.

* The rate at which MRB authority may be converted for use in MCC programs is increased to 25 percent from 20 percent.

* The sunset date for MCCs is extended one year to December 31, 1988.

Multifamily Bonds:

Tighter Income Caps

* Multifamily rental projects that are financed with tax-exempt funds must reserve either 20 percent of the units for tenants earning 50 percent or less of area median income (adjusted for family size), or 40 percent of the units for persons with incomes of 60 percent or less of area median income (adjusted for family size). Previously, bond-financed projects were required to set aside 20 percent of units for tenants earning 80 percent or less of area median income (adjusted for family size).

New Tax Credit

* Projects financed with tax-exempt bonds are eligible for another major subsidy, a low-income rental housing tax credit of 4 percent annually for ten years (see Chapter 6). The credits are available automatically to tax-exempt financed projects, without going through the credit allocation process.

**Mortgage credit certificates (MCCs) provide eligible home buyers with a credit to reduce their annual Federal tax liability. The credit is equal to a percentage of home buyers' mortgage interest payments. MCCs may only be issued if a state's MRB authority has been traded in for that purpose.

Longer Commitment Period

* Projects must meet low-income set-aside requirements for at least 15 years, up from 10 years under the old rules.

Provisions Affecting Investors in Tax-Exempt Bonds

The tax bill contains several provisions that affect demand for tax-exempt securities and should affect the relative cost of borrowing for certain types of tax-exempt bonds, including housing bonds:

* Lower marginal tax rates may boost investor yield requirements on tax-exempt securities relative to comparable taxable instruments.

* Interest income from all new issues of private-activity bonds (except 501(c)(3) issues) is treated as a preference item that is added to taxable income for purposes of determining the alternative minimum tax for individuals.

* For corporations, the calculation of their alternative minimum tax requires firms to add to taxable income one-half of the difference between taxable and book income. Tax-exempt interest from all bonds, regardless of issue date, is counted in book income.

* Financial institutions may no longer deduct 80 percent of the interest they pay on funds invested in most tax-exempt securities.

* Property and casualty insurance companies must reduce their deduction for loss reserves by 15 percent of their interest income on tax-exempt bonds.

At present, the uncertain future supply of tax-exempt securities makes it difficult to assess the impact of these impediments to demand on the cost of borrowing on housing and other private-activity bonds. The change in institutional demand seems likely to have the greatest impact, with a sharp fall off in bank purchases pushing up tax-exempt yields in the shorter and intermediate maturities, where most bank activity occurs, producing a flattening of the tax-exempt yield curve. In terms of housing this will raise rates for short-term, rollover bonds, called "lower floaters", issued for multifamily projects.

The alternative minimum tax provisions should raise investors' required yield relative to alternative taxable investments and are likely to produce a multi-tiered market, where private-activity issues carry a yield premium over public-use tax-exempt securities. The diminished supply of municipal securities, the loss of most other tax shelters, and the phase-in of the lower tax rates, however, could diffuse somewhat pressures for higher relative tax-exempt yields. In the near term, the overall result of the tax changes seems likely to leave longer-term tax-exempt rates at levels fairly close to historical relationships--80 percent of rates on similar taxable bonds.

Prospects for Tax-Exempt Financing

Uncertainty over the effective dates of bond provisions on the tax reform bill has hampered housing finance agency operations throughout 1986. Most agencies are only now reviewing options and formulating strategies for operating in the post-tax reform era. The most pressing uncertainty is the amount of tax-exempt bond authority that will be available for housing issuers and the distribution of that authority among state and local agencies. That allocation must be determined by the governor and legislature in each state.

Mortgage Revenue Bonds. The tax bill's impact should be less severe in the single-family area. Agencies have had success this year in recycling their home loan funds through "current refundings" of bonds that were issued in earlier years when interest rates were higher. By using the prepayments on the high rate mortgages from the older programs to call the related outstanding issues, agencies can, in effect, refinance those bonds at the current lower rates and avoid the new volume limitations and targeting rules. Current refundings should continue to serve as a source of MRB funds as long as interest rates remain near or below current levels. Relatively restrained demand for MRB funds, due to the reduced borrowing costs and ample supply of non-subsidized loans, should also help housing finance agencies maintain their MRB programs.

The targeting requirements for single family programs should not prove to be disruptive in most states, as long as mortgage borrowing costs remain near or below the relatively low levels experienced during most of 1986. At higher mortgage rate levels, however, the income restrictions become a significant hindrance to activity in the majority of states. Exhibit 5.3 shows that, as interest rates rise, persons with incomes meeting the new MRB rules will find it more difficult to qualify for a mortgage loan, even on many moderately-priced homes within the revised MRB sales price limits.

The problem is more pronounced for buyers seeking new homes, because those homes generally carry higher price tags than comparable existing units. In more than half of the states, interest rates over 13 percent would limit persons meeting the new income restrictions to purchasing new homes priced at less than 80 percent of the revised MRB sales price limit. This circumstance will greatly reduce the new construction element of housing finance agency programs whenever interest rates move higher.

The bill provides one additional year of MRB authority (through 1988), but the volume limitations will be more restrictive in 1988. The increase in the conversion rate for mortgage credit certificates may not be significant, since conversions will be dampened because authorities are able to carry forward unused bond authority and the competition for funds under the unified volume cap will greatly reduce the supply of excess bond authority. In addition, the Tax Act reduces the number of households with qualifying incomes that also have sufficient tax liability to utilize the credit.

with qualifying incomes that also have sufficient tax liability to utilize the credit.

Multifamily IDBs. Multifamily programs will fare much worse under the new tax rules. This is mostly due to the sharp reduction in tax advantages to rental housing in general (see Chapter 2). The stricter low-income set-aside requirements would, by themselves, greatly reduce the number of projects that would pencil out. However, the low-income rental tax credit should fully offset the costs of meeting the tighter targeting (see Chapter 6). Agencies already have experienced a sharp fall-off in their multifamily rental programs and have been unable to disburse all of the bulge of project funds that were raised in the latter months of 1985.

Other Responses. With the new volume restrictions and targeting requirements, most agencies probably will scale back the range and scope of their programs, with greater cutbacks in the multifamily area than in single family programs. Agencies are likely to increasingly utilize a patchwork of financing sources. Tax-exempt financing will continue to be employed, but the volume and targeting limitations on this traditional channel will require agencies to rely more heavily on alternate sources of funds. Housing finance agencies have long used various federal programs and will continue to do so, though the federal contribution will continue to diminish. The recent trend toward greater reliance on state programs and funding should pick up steam as states and localities attempt to meet affordable housing needs in the wake of cutbacks at the federal level. State and local contributions will come through housing trust funds, direct grants, general obligation funding, and appropriations from other revenue sources. States and localities also may provide housing incentives through tax provisions, regulatory easements and redevelopment programs. To obtain state and local funds, agencies may be required to bolster their "public purpose" stance by focusing their programs to an even greater degree on lower income participants.

To avoid the cap on private activity bonds, agencies will continue to refinance outstanding issues and will increase issues of taxable bonds. Some agencies may seek to retain ownership of rental projects, with the developer building the structure on a turnkey basis, in order to tap the unlimited supply of public-use tax-exempt bonds. Revolving loan funds, where a pool of loans provides backing for a series of financings, will be another technique used to stretch limited bond authority. Some agencies may be able to draw upon reserves and other assets, such as land holdings, to structure deals that will work with more limited tax-exempt bond resources.

In summary, housing finance agencies should continue to function in the post-tax-reform era, but most programs should operate on a smaller scale, and will, by law and state policy, be more targeted to low income participants. Funding will take on an even more patchwork structure, combining tax-exempt and taxable bonds with low-income housing tax credits, remaining federal assistance and a growing repertoire of state and local resources and initiatives. The availablility of financing and the degree of change in agency programs will vary widely across the country, depending on agencies' financial condition and the degree of housing commitment on the part of state and local government.

EXHIBIT 5.3

THE EFFECT OF MRB INCOME LIMITS ON MORTGAGE QUALIFICATION

STATE	115% OF MEDIAN FAMILY INCOME	MAXIMUM AFFORDABLE SALES PRICE 5% DOWN @ 9%	MAXIMUM AFFORDABLE SALES PRICE 5% DOWN @ 13%	MRB PURCHASE PRICE LIMIT FOR NEW HOMES	AFFORDABLE PRICE AS A % OF PURCHASE PRICE LIMIT @ 9%	@ 13%
ALABAMA	$25,875	$72,286	$53,823	$69,648	104%	77%
ALASKA	$47,610	$138,823	$102,225	$120,426	115%	85%
ARIZONA	$28,635	$77,747	$58,308	$93,416	83%	62%
ARKANSAS	$23,575	$60,600	$46,062	$63,926	95%	72%
CALIFORNIA	$35,190	$92,495	$69,927	$118,582	78%	59%
COLORADO	$33,350	$88,489	$66,744	$105,063	84%	64%
CONNECTICUT	$39,675	$113,790	$84,155	$97,086	117%	87%
DELAWARE	$34,615	$93,530	$70,230	$90,869	103%	77%
DISTRICT OF COLUMBIA	$47,955	$124,643	$94,488	$126,013	99%	75%
FLORIDA	$29,440	$78,337	$59,046	$73,814	106%	80%
GEORGIA	$29,670	$77,189	$58,501	$84,119	92%	70%
HAWAII	$34,730	$95,312	$71,290	$142,148	67%	50%
IDAHO	$26,220	$69,112	$52,214	$75,317	92%	69%
ILLINOIS	$36,685	$90,719	$69,589	$91,123	100%	76%
INDIANA	$31,625	$81,743	$62,050	$66,565	123%	93%
IOWA	$31,395	$77,981	$59,757	$66,317	118%	90%
KANSAS	$32,085	$84,731	$63,984	$78,234	108%	82%
KENTUCKY	$25,530	$67,294	$50,840	$69,434	97%	73%
LOUISIANA	$30,015	$86,262	$63,762	$71,918	120%	89%
MAINE	$27,025	$68,032	$51,969	$62,610	109%	83%
MARYLAND	$38,755	$98,805	$75,249	$90,405	109%	83%
MASSACHUSETTS	$35,650	$87,159	$67,035	$90,329	96%	74%
MICHIGAN	$33,580	$76,550	$59,809	$76,529	100%	78%
MINNESOTA	$34,385	$92,108	$69,311	$88,409	104%	78%
MISSISSIPPI	$23,230	$62,406	$46,927	$76,732	81%	61%
MISSOURI	$30,475	$79,802	$60,386	$81,396	98%	74%
MONTANA	$27,485	$71,438	$54,155	NA	NA	NA
NEBRASKA	$30,820	$73,614	$56,921	$73,234	101%	78%
NEVADA	$32,660	$88,934	$66,650	$75,844	117%	88%
NEW HAMPSHIRE	$34,500	$81,638	$63,259	$88,772	92%	71%
NEW JERSEY	$38,295	$88,305	$68,820	$93,166	95%	74%
NEW MEXICO	$26,220	$69,902	$52,663	$70,538	99%	75%
NEW YORK	$33,925	$77,463	$60,501	$89,518	87%	68%
NORTH CAROLINA	$28,060	$74,383	$56,117	$69,683	107%	81%
NORTH DAKOTA	$28,865	$74,403	$56,516	$51,543	144%	110%
OHIO	$31,970	$83,250	$63,081	$76,104	109%	83%
OKLAHOMA	$30,705	$81,937	$61,716	$73,628	111%	84%
OREGON	$30,705	$72,413	$56,153	$74,552	97%	75%
PENNSYLVANIA	$31,970	$79,129	$60,686	$72,644	109%	84%
RHODE ISLAND	$32,200	$77,639	$59,904	$73,045	106%	82%
SOUTH CAROLINA	$28,290	$75,781	$57,025	$78,558	96%	73%
SOUTH DAKOTA	$25,300	$62,399	$47,895	NA	NA	NA
TENNESSEE	$26,335	$68,449	$51,889	$67,839	101%	76%
TEXAS	$32,775	$83,711	$63,726	$92,692	90%	69%
UTAH	$34,500	$91,367	$68,947	$80,552	113%	86%
VERMONT	$28,405	$82,825	$60,989	NA	NA	NA
VIRGINIA	$34,270	$88,173	$67,005	$73,135	121%	92%
WASHINGTON	$33,235	$87,521	$66,136	$84,787	103%	78%
WEST VIRGINIA	$28,060	$76,408	$57,262	NA	NA	NA
WISCONSIN	$32,085	$78,102	$60,130	$76,974	101%	78%
WYOMING	$33,120	$92,250	$68,741	NA	NA	NA

Assumptions:
30 year term, 5% downpayment,
28% PITI/income underwriting.
NA: Not available due to insufficient sample size.

SOURCE:
Median family incomes from revised HUD estimates for FY1986.
Taxes and insurance based on FHA experience.
Average area purchase prices from IRS Bulletin #1985-33.

BUILDER BONDS

The Tax Act also severely reduces the tax benefits that have been available to home builders who provide financing for their customers. Under the former tax rules, builder-financed sales of homes could be accounted for using the installment method, where the builder-holder of the mortgage defers tax on the sales profit until loan payments are received over the life of the mortgage. Builders issuing bonds collateralized by mortgages were able to obtain cash shortly after the sale of their homes, but could spread tax payments on those sales over a number of years. Builder bond volume grew rapidly from the first issue in 1979, totaling more than $5 billion in 1985 and approaching $7 billion this year (see Exhibit 5.4).

Use of installment sales accounting is generally curtailed under the new tax law. Holders of mortgages and other installment receivables now must apply a complicated formula, called the "proportionate disallowance rule," to determine what percentage of future loan repayments are subject to tax in the current year. The rule treats a portion of a builder's liabilities as payments received on mortgage holdings, regardless of whether the mortgages are specifically pledged as collateral.

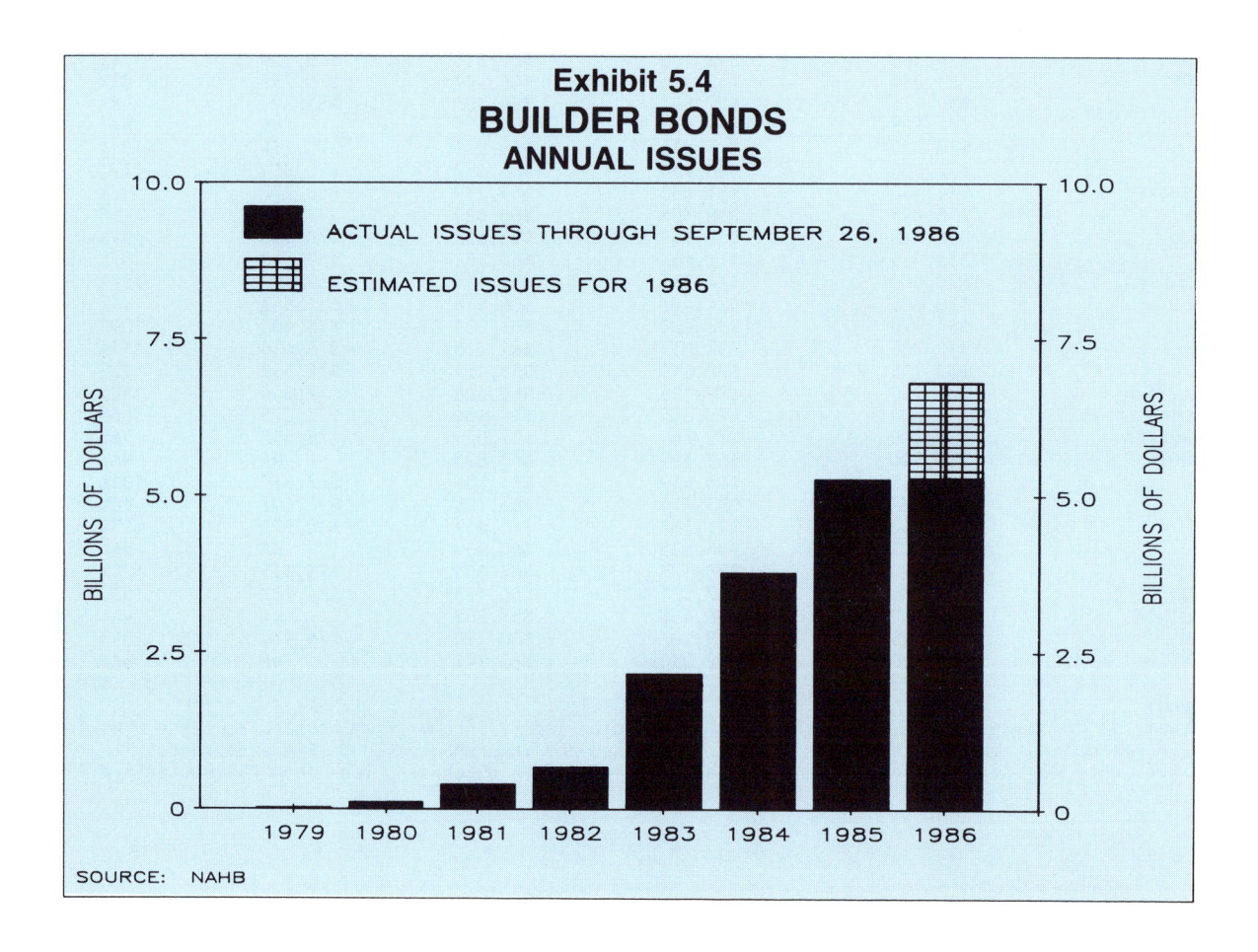

Exhibit 5.4
BUILDER BONDS
ANNUAL ISSUES

SOURCE: NAHB

The calculation involves dividing the firm's average indebtedness for the year by the sum of all installment receivables and the adjusted basis of all other assets, then multiplying the result by mortgages outstanding (which were originated after February 28, 1986). This "allocable installment indebtedness" (less the portion taxed in earlier years) is the amount treated as a payment on the builder's mortgage holdings. The formula means that the smaller a builder's equity, or, conversely, the higher the ratio of debt (including mortgage-backed bonds) to assets (including mortgage holdings), then the greater the proportion of mortgage loans that must be treated as if payment had been received in that tax year. For most builders, the ratio will be close to 1.0.

The installment sales provision is effective for tax years ending after December 31, 1986. Mortgages from sales made after February 28, 1986 must be included in the proportionate disallowance calculation. However, builder bond issuers are permitted an important transition exception. In the first year under the new provisions, allocable installment indebtedness may be spread evenly over that period and the two following years. In the second year, the alloted payments may be divided between that year and the next year. The provision becomes fully effective in the third tax year after December 31, 1986. While they are brief, these deferrals will carry a portion of profits to the new lower rates of 1988.

The new rule effectively eliminates tax deferral for the majority of builder bond issuers and sharply limits the amount of deferral for those still able to postpone some tax liability. The proportionate disallowance rule will reverse the trend toward greater builder involvement in home financing. Some home builders will continue to originate mortgage loans for their customers, but such activity will be limited to larger firms that operate mortgage banking subsidiaries. Most of these builders will not retain ownership of their new home loans, since they will no longer have a tax incentive to put the loans on their books.

THRIFT INSTITUTIONS

Thrift institutions (savings and loan associations and mutual savings banks) make the majority of the nation's home mortgage loans. As shown in Exhibit 5.5 thrifts originated more than half of all home loans last year and held over 40 percent of all home mortgages outstanding (excluding mortgage securities). The deep involvement of these institutions in home lending has been encouraged by a lengthy history of legislative and regulatory requirements and inducements.

One of the major incentives to thrift housing investment is the special bad debt reserve tax deduction, which allows savings and loan associations and mutual savings banks to reduce their taxable income if a required percentage of their assets is in housing related investments. The new tax law reduces both the amount of the deduction, to eight percent from 40 percent of taxable income, and the percentage of assets that must be held in the form of mortgages, to 60 percent from 82 percent for S&Ls and 72 percent for savings banks. The change probably will not cause a major shift in the thrift share of mortgage lending, since S&Ls and savings banks are likely to continue to pursue familiar channels of business. Even so, thrifts will sell more of their loan originations, reducing their holdings of home loans and diversifying their portfolios into other assets.

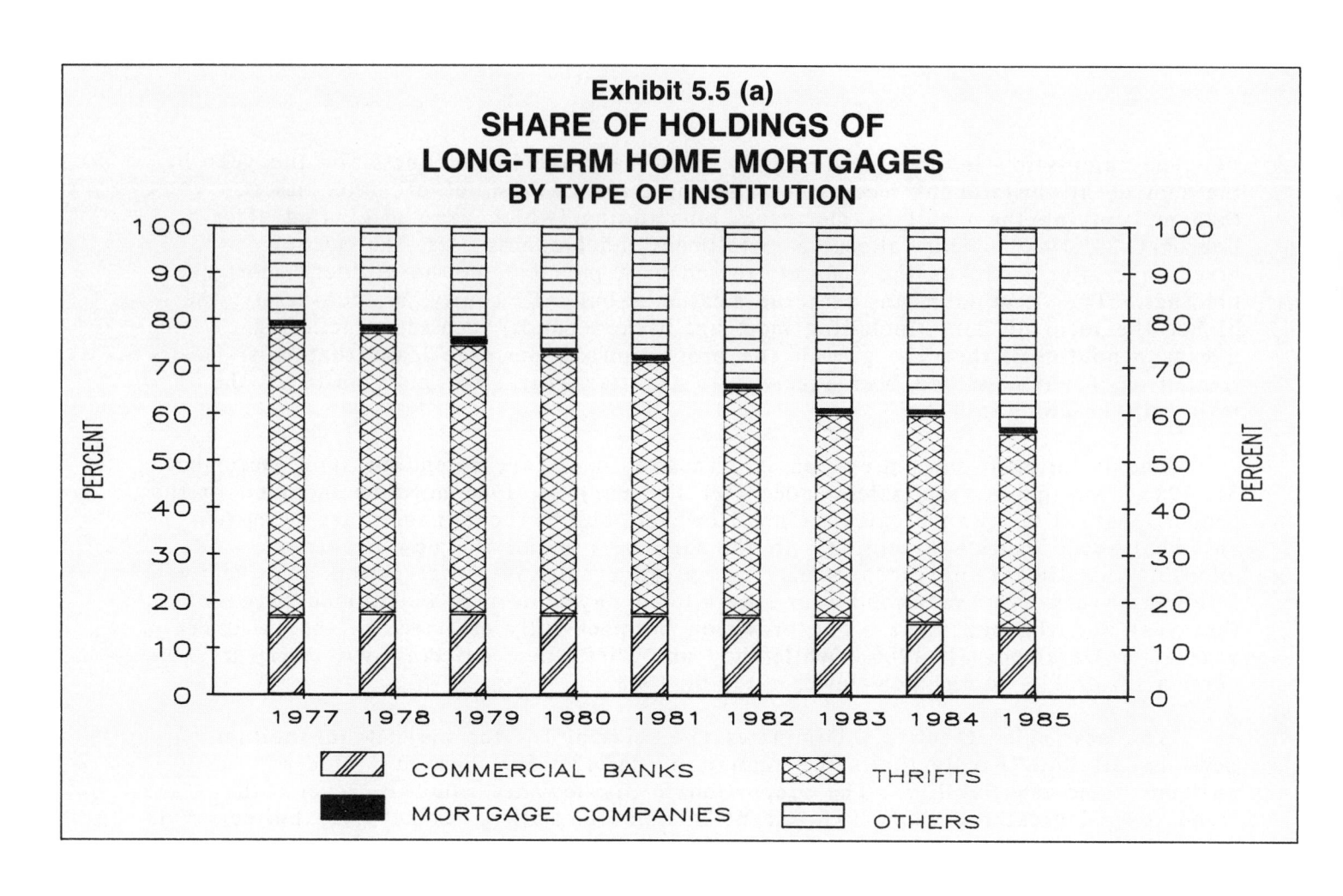

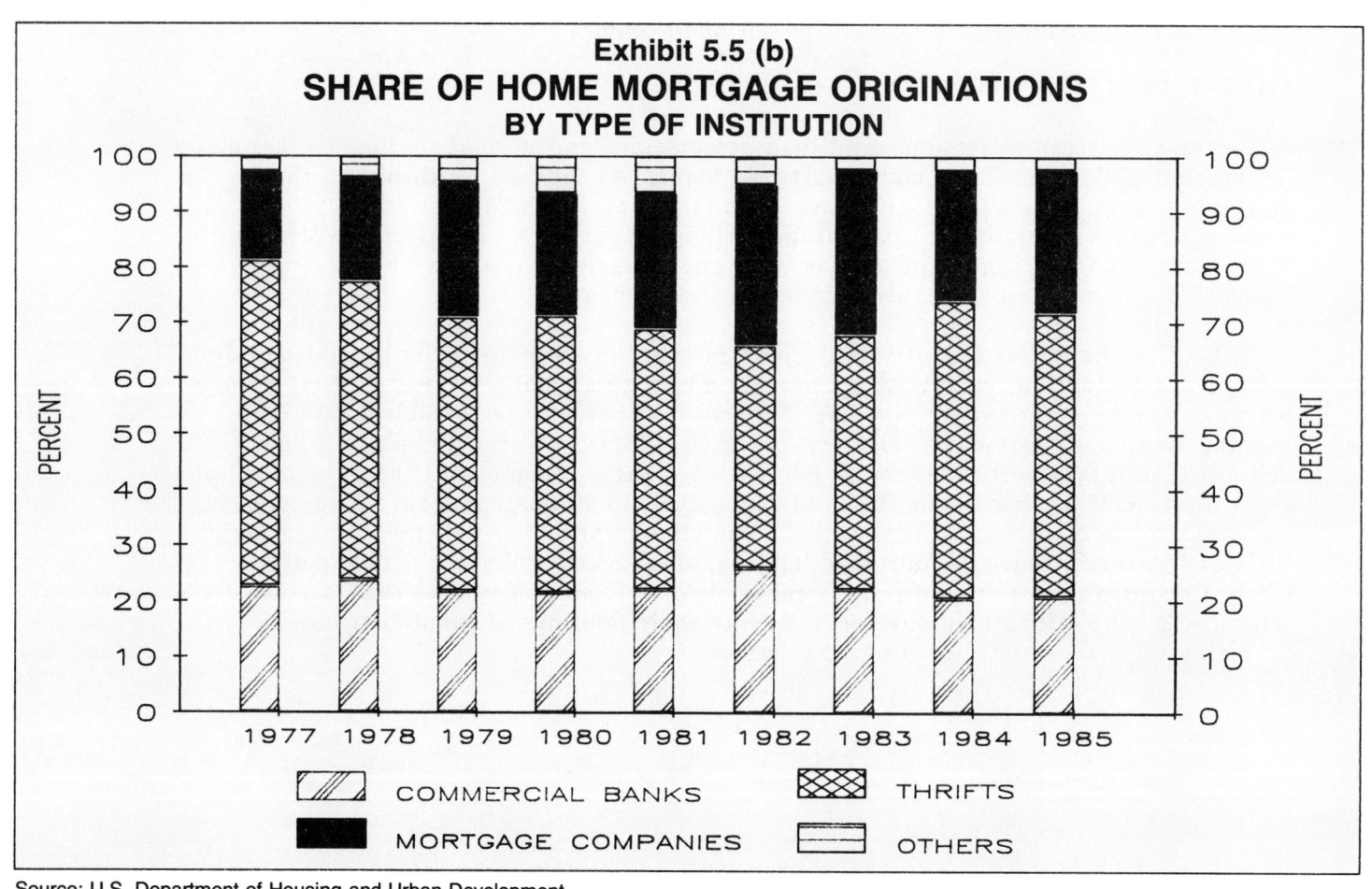

Exhibit 5.5 (a)
SHARE OF HOLDINGS OF LONG-TERM HOME MORTGAGES
BY TYPE OF INSTITUTION

- COMMERCIAL BANKS
- THRIFTS
- MORTGAGE COMPANIES
- OTHERS

Exhibit 5.5 (b)
SHARE OF HOME MORTGAGE ORIGINATIONS
BY TYPE OF INSTITUTION

- COMMERCIAL BANKS
- THRIFTS
- MORTGAGE COMPANIES
- OTHERS

Source: U.S. Department of Housing and Urban Development.

MULTIPLE CLASS MORTGAGE SECURITIES (REMICs vs. CMOs)

The Real Estate Mortgage Investment Conduit (REMIC) provision of the Tax Act opens a new avenue of possibilities for sales of mortgages in security form. A REMIC holds a pool of mortgage loans and issues securities representing interests in those mortgages. This new entity enables a pool of mortgages to offer ownership interests in a range of maturities, with greater choice as to the length of investment. The REMIC provision also contains rules to reduce confusion in the taxation of mortgage-backed securities.

The use of the securities markets to sell mortgages began more than a decade and a half ago with the development of mortgage pass-through securities. These securities provided investors with payments of principal and interest on the pooled loans without the administrative burden associated with direct holdings of mortgage obligations. Under a special provision of tax law, these pools are exempt from corporate income tax. However, the requirements for such exemption include a rule that all investors in the pool have equal claim on the income stream. Purchasers of pass-through mortgage securities, like holders of raw mortgages, actually own a combination of short-term and long-term assets due to the risk that their investment will mature ahead of schedule as a result of homeowners paying off their mortgage loans early to move or obtain a lower mortgage rate.

Mortgage-backed securities structured in more than one maturity class were developed to provide investors with greater call protection on their securities by directing loan prepayments to the holders of the shortest maturity classes. Under previous tax rules, unfortunately, the multiple class structure was restricted to mortgage-backed debt, called collateralized mortgage obligations or CMOs, and was not permitted for issuers wishing to sell their mortgage loans in the form of pools. (Exhibit 5.6 shows the rapid expansion of CMO issues since their inception in 1983.)

The creation of REMICs enables issuers of "sale of assets" securities to obtain the higher prices that investors offer for the greater degree of call protection and choice of maturities in multiclass instruments. Issuers also are able to take advantage of lower interest rates in the shorter end of the market. Unlike CMOs, REMICs do not require issuers to retain equity in an offering, increasing the percentage of proceeds that are obtained from the sale of a mortgage pool. In addition, the flexible REMIC framework may assume a variety of legal and accounting treatments and will accommodate other innovations in the structure of mortgage-backed securities. In that regard, REMICs may be popular among large-scale builders as a source of builder financing.

The availability of a flexible and efficient vehicle for mortgage sales in multiple maturity classes should have a major influence on the way mortgages are traded in the secondary market. REMICs also should affect the composition of investors in mortgages and the form in which home loans are held. Under the former tax rules, the requirement that multiclass mortgage securities be in debt form made it difficult for many mortgage market participants to become issuers. Mortgage bankers and Wall Street firms will become major players in the new instrument, now that the securities offerings will not burden the liability side of their balance

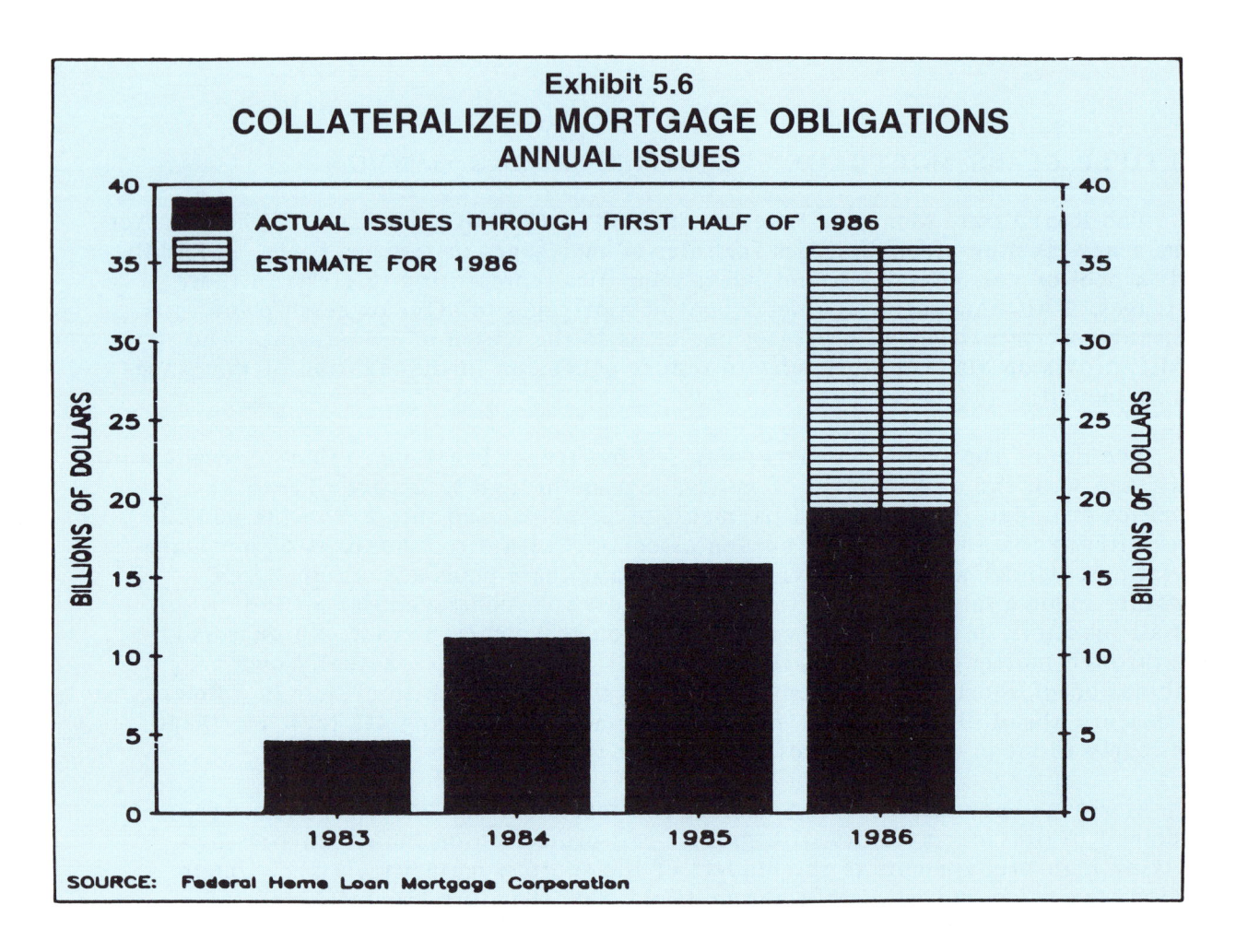

**Exhibit 5.6
COLLATERALIZED MORTGAGE OBLIGATIONS
ANNUAL ISSUES**

SOURCE: Federal Home Loan Mortgage Corporation

sheets. The Federal National Mortgage Association (Fannie Mae) and the Federal Home Loan Mortgage Corporation (Freddie Mac) are permitted to issue REMIC securities and the single-class pass-through securities of Fannie Mae and Freddie Mac may be used in multi-class REMIC mortgage pools.

On the investor side, REMICs will provide security structures and maturities that will be attractive to a broad range of purchasers. Sales of shorter maturities have been popular in overseas markets, and such activity will be boosted by the liberalization of tax withholding rules for foreign investors in REMIC mortgages. Thrift institutions also will purchase the short maturity ranges as part of efforts to better match assets and liabilities. REMIC securities are treated as qualifying mortgage assets for purposes of the thrift bad debt reserve tax deduction. The securities are also eligible assets for real estate investment trusts, and these entities will join pension funds as purchasers of longer REMIC maturities.

These changes will produce an improved mortgage delivery system. REMIC securities will aid efforts to broaden the investor base for mortgages and will permit issuers to gain greater proceeds from their mortgage sales. While some of the pricing and marketing benefits previously shown by CMOs may be offset by a heavy volume of REMIC offerings, the securities still should produce a net reduction in the cost of home mortgage loans. Initial estimates are that rates on fixed-rate loans might be lowered by 25 basis points.

Chapter 6

THE LOW-INCOME RENTAL HOUSING CREDIT

Douglas B. Diamond, Jr.
Assistant Staff Vice President for Housing Policy
National Association of Home Builders

One of the few areas of real estate development for which Congress showed any tangible concern was low- and moderate-income housing. Although the jury is still out on how successfully the Act will maintain investment in such housing, the new provisions in this area are worth close examination by both developers and owners of existing properties.

Until the 1986 Act, tax law was used to foster low- and moderate-income housing primarily in tandem with non-tax assistance programs. Prior law provided qualifying low-income projects with tax benefits greater than those for other rental housing, including more rapid depreciation, expensing of construction period interest and taxes, and more favorable recapture at time of sale. In general, these tax benefits were intended to provide investors with an acceptable rate of return on projects in which cash returns were unlikely or limited by contract. However, they did not provide, by themselves, sufficient subsidy to permit the construction of rental housing for very low-income households.

Even if these provisions had been kept intact, and the additional direct subsidies were provided, other changes in the new tax law would have rendered them ineffective in causing lower-income housing to be constructed or rehabilitated. The approach of providing deep tax shelters was too weakened by the drop in tax rates, by the end of a capital gains rate differential, and by the passive loss limitation. Thus an entirely new approach to subsidizing low-income housing was created, one that attempts not only to match the previous incentives but to even provide through the tax code the deep subsidies needed to construct housing for the poor. The new subsidy is called the low-income rental housing credit.

THE BASICS OF THE CREDIT

Exhibit 6.1 summarizes the major provisions of the credit. Actually, there are three different credits, depending on whether the housing is to be constructed, rehabilitated or simply acquired, and on whether other federal subsidies are involved. The largest credit is for up to 9 percent of the depreciable basis of the qualifying units for new construction or for expenditures on the rehabilitation of existing units. This 9 percent credit is for each year for ten years, for a total of 90 percent of the depreciable expenditures. The basis is not reduced by the amount of the credit.

New construction and rehabilitation expenditures which benefit from a subsidized federal loan or tax-exempt financing are not eligible for receiving the 9 percent credit. Instead, they are eligible for a 4 percent annual credit.

Exhibit 6.1
Summary of the Low-Income Rental Housing Credit

Categories of Eligible Projects:	Maximum Credit
1. **New Construction and Rehabilitation of Existing Housing** *only on rehabilitation or construction expenditures, not acquisition costs. *only on expenditures on qualifying units, not other units.	9%
2. **New Construction and Rehabilitation Financed by a Subsidized Federal Loan or a Tax-exempt Bond** *e.g., FmHA Section 515 projects. *assistance derived from federal grants such as from CDBG or UDAG is not treated as a federal subsidy.	4%
3. **Acquisition Cost of Existing Housing** *includes all federally assisted projects. *this can be used with the other two credits for doing rehabilitation. *projects must not have been placed in service previously within 10 years (may be waived for troubled projects.)	4%

State Volume Limitation
*state can issue credits equal to $1.25 per resident.
*state credit authority is not needed for projects financed by tax exempt bonds.
*10 percent of authority must be reserved for certain non-profit organizations.

Allocation Procedures
*states can choose any allocation process.
*credits are applied against the allocation for the year in which the property is placed in service.

Targeting Requirements
*20 percent (40 percent) or more of units in projects must be occupied by individuals who have incomes of 50 percent (60 percent) or less of area median income, adjusted for family size.
*adjustments for extremely high housing costs or low incomes may be made in a manner consistent with HUD's Section 8 program.

Rent Restrictions
*gross rent paid by families in qualifying units, including an allowance for utilities, may not exceed 30 percent of the applicable qualifying income for a family of its size.

Period of Credit
*10 years

Recapture Provisions
*if income targeting for a qualifying unit is not met in a specific year, the "accelerated" credit amounts for that unit for earlier years are recaptured, with interest.
*if minimum income targeting for the project is not met at any time during the first 10 years, the "accelerated" portion (generally one-third) of **all** credit amounts is recaptured. This recapture is phased out between years 11 and 15.

Investor Limitations
*in general, investors in qualifying projects are limited in the amount of credit they can apply to taxes and the amount of losses they can deduct. The total of losses plus credits can have an aggregate effect of reducing taxable income by $25,000 or taxes by $7,000. This amount is expanded by the amount of any net income received from qualifying passive investments. The loss amount is phased out at incomes between $100,000 and $150,000. The credit amount is phased out at incomes between $200,000 and $250,000.

Sunset
*Projects must either be completed by 12/31/89, or 10 percent completed by 12/31/88 and put in service by 12/31/90.

Effective Date
*January 1, 1987

Existing projects, whether federally assisted or not, also are eligible for a
4 percent credit upon resale if they have not been placed in service within the
previous ten years (in general, "placed in service" refers to the receipt of the
initial occupancy permit or a change of ownership).

For a project to qualify for the credit, certain set-asides for low-income
residents must be maintained. A project must set-aside a minimum of either 20
percent of the units for households with incomes of 50 percent or less of area median
income, as adjusted for family size, or 40 percent of the units for households with
incomes of 60 percent or less of area median income, adjusted for family size. Given
that these minimums have been met, the share of the project that qualifies for the
credit generally depends on the share of the units whose residents meet the same
income cut-off as was used to establish project eligibility. Unoccupied units are
assumed to be non-qualifying unless previously occupied by a qualifying household.
In addition, gross rents for a qualifying unit cannot exceed 30 percent of the
maximum qualifying income for the family size in that unit.

In general, if a project utilizes the credit, it must continue to meet the
minimum set-aside requirements for 15 years (as is the case for tax-exempt financed
projects under the Act). Failure to meet the requirements during the first ten years
results in recapture of a third of all credits taken, plus interest. This potential
for recapture is then phased out over the following five years.

The credit is not an entitlement in general. An eligible project must receive
an allocation of the credit through an allocation process set up by each state. An
important exception is projects that are funded through tax-exempt bonds issued
after August 15, 1986 and thus subject to the new volume cap on private-activity
bonds. Such projects do not then also have to draw upon the credit volume cap. Ten
percent of the credit allocation must be set aside for non-profit organizations whose
purpose is to foster low-income housing.

Some specific examples may help clarify some of the uses of the credit. One use
might be combining the credit with tax-exempt financing to do a moderate-income new
construction project of the type commonly built with tax-exempt bonds in 1985. Tax-
exempt financing will require the same tight income targeting as the credit if built
under the new law and will have to vie for an allocation of bond authority, but it
may also be entitled to the 4 percent credit on its set-aside units.

Another example is an existing six-flat building in an inner-city neighborhood
in which all units are occupied by households with qualifying incomes. The purchaser
of such a building is eligible to apply for a 4 percent credit on its entire
depreciable basis if the building's date of construction or last resale is ten years
or more prior to this resale. If rehabilitation expenditures are then made, those
expenditures would be eligible for a 9 percent credit if they received no "federal
assistance."

Existing federally assisted projects would be treated the same as other existing
buildings. It is important to note, though, that in all cases except that of the
tax-exempt financed projects, the owner must seek an allocation of the credit through
the state-determined allocation process.

The credit authority itself first becomes available in 1987 and sunsets at the end of 1989, except for projects for which 10 percent or more of total project costs are incurred before 1989 and the project is placed in service before 1991. Thus there is no assurance that such credits will be available at time of resale of an eligible project.

SOME OF THE DETAILS

A full discussion of all of the technical and financial issues, and the rules and exceptions to the rules, involved with the low-income housing credit is beyond the scope of this report. The Statement of Managers of the Conference Committee (Volume II of the Conference Report) provides an extensive summary and explanation that should be read carefully. Some issues will have no answers until further guidance is forthcoming from the staff of the Joint Committee on Taxation or from the Treasury. However, most of the important complexities can be discussed briefly here.

Credit Percentages

Perhaps the most basic complexity is that the credit percentages will be different for projects placed in service after 1987. Projects receiving credits in 1987 will continue to receive the same amount annually. Similarly, a project placed in service in July of 1988, for example, will thereafter for 10 years receive a constant amount. However, that amount will be determined in July 1988, based on interest rates at that time. The purpose is to keep the present value of the credit the same, no matter what might happen to interest rates.

After 1987, the 9 percent credit will be transformed into a percentage such that the present value of 10 years of the credit will equal 70 percent of the initial depreciable basis. The calculation will be made using the average interest rate on medium- and long-term federal debt, adjusted for a 28 percent tax rate. This after-tax discount rate will be much lower than actual discount rates applied by investors to the credit, but both the official discount rate and investor rates should move together. Thus, if interest rates rise by 1988 because of fears of higher inflation or other reasons, the actual percentage rate for the credit will probably be higher than 9 percent. For example, if Treasury bond rates are 10 percent in July 1988, then the relevant discount rate used will be 7.2 percent and the credit rate will be 10.1 percent.

The same rules apply to the 4 percent credit, which will be based on a present value of 30 percent. The credit amount will vary on a monthly basis, but, as noted, the credit percentage will stay constant for ten years once set for a project at the time it is placed in service. Developers will not know the nominal amount of the credit at the time the project is started, but will be protected at least partially from changes in interest rates over the course of development.

Credit Allocations

Note that, since a project becomes eligible for the credits only at the time it is placed in service, the allocation to the project through the state allocation process applies against the credit limits applicable to the year the project is placed in service. Presumably, a project will be able to secure a commitment of credits from the credit allocation body before beginning construction.

Only certain aspects of the state credit allocation process are known at this time. First, the annual credit limit for each state is an amount equal to $1.25 per resident of the state as estimated by the Census for the previous year. This amount is the total in annual credit amounts allocated to projects placed in service that year (i.e., this is the annual amount, not the present value of the credit amounts for all ten years). Exhibit 6.2 shows estimates of the amount of credits available by state in 1987. The number of units that can receive credits depends on the split between the 9 percent and 4 percent credit uses that a state follows. (In addition, projects financed with tax-exempt bonds are eligible for credits outside of the volume cap.) Unused credit authority cannot be carried over to the next year. The credit allocation body is encouraged to reduce the credit amount below the maximum permitted for a project if they judge the project to be feasible without the maximum credits.

Exhibit 6.2
Estimated Annual State Ceilings For Low-Income Rental Housing Tax Credits*

State	Population 1985 Est. (millions)	Ceiling for Low-Income Rental Tax Credits (millions $)	State	Population 1985 Est. (millions)	Ceiling for Low-Income Rental Tax Credits (millions $)
Alabama	4.021	$ 5.026	Montana	0.826	$ 1.033
Alaska	0.521	0.651	Nebraska	1.606	2.008
Arizona	3.187	3.984	Nevada	0.936	1.170
Arkansas	2.359	2.949	New Hampshire	0.998	1.248
California	26.365	32.956	New Jersey	7.562	9.453
Colorado	3.231	4.039	New Mexico	1.450	1.813
Connecticut	3.174	3.968	New York	17.783	22.229
Delaware	0.622	0.778	North Carolina	6.255	7.819
District of Columbia	0.626	0.783	North Dakota	0.685	0.856
Florida	11.366	14.208	Ohio	10.744	13.430
Georgia	5.976	7.470	Oklahoma	3.301	4.126
Hawaii	1.054	1.318	Oregon	2.687	3.359
Idaho	1.005	1.256	Pennsylvania	11.853	14.816
Illinois	11.535	14.419	Rhode Island	0.968	1.210
Indiana	5.499	6.874	South Carolina	3.347	4.184
Iowa	2.884	3.605	South Dakota	0.708	0.885
Kansas	2.450	3.063	Tennessee	4.762	5.953
Kentucky	3.726	4.658	Texas	16.370	20.463
Louisiana	4.481	5.601	Utah	1.645	2.056
Maine	1.164	1.455	Vermont	0.535	0.669
Maryland	4.392	5.490	Virginia	5.706	7.133
Massachusetts	5.822	7.278	Washington	4.409	5.511
Michigan	9.088	11.360	West Virginia	1.936	2.420
Minnesota	4.193	5.241	Wisconsin	4.775	5.969
Mississippi	2.613	3.266	Wyoming	0.509	0.636
Missouri	5.029	6.286	TOTAL	238.739	$298.424

*State ceilings are based on Census Bureau provisional population estimates for July 1985.

The Act provides three general allocation procedures to be followed by states. First, the entire allocation authority falls to the "state housing agency," which may include more than one agency. Second, the governor can instead allocate the authority among all of the governmental units and other issuing authorities. Last, the state legislature can overrule the governor to provide its own allocation of authority.

A critical question is whether the demand for the credit will far exceed the available supply. If it does, difficult choices will have to be made by the allocation authorities and much effort may have to be expended by a developer to secure the credits. It appears that the single most important determinant of how readily available the credit will be is the level of use of the credit for acquisitions, particularly of existing, unassisted low-income housing.

At one extreme, if all of the credits were used for new construction with an average depreciable basis of $40,000 per unit, the $300 million in credits available for the whole country would permit 83,333 units to receive 9 percent credits, a greater number of new units than HUD has subsidized in any year since 1981. Alternatively, if all the allocation was used for rehabilitation expenditures averaging $20,000 per unit, twice as many units could be authorized. Both of these numbers are probably large compared to the total number of units ordinarily constructed or rehabilitated for low-income households (although state-to-state variation in activity may be significant). Finally, if all the allocation was used for acquisitions of existing buildings at an average depreciable basis of $20,000 per unit, 375,000 units could be funded with the 4 percent credit. But this number may be relatively small compared to the annual transactions in eligible existing projects.

Qualified Basis

The dollar amount against which the credit percentage is applied is called the "qualified basis." The qualified basis is a proportion of what is called the "eligible basis," where the proportion is the lesser of (1) the proportion of the number of low-income units to all residential units or (2) the proportion of the floor space of the low-income units to that of all residential rental units.

In general, the "eligible" basis against which the proportion is applied consists of the adjusted basis of (1) the new construction costs, (2) the cost of rehabilitation, or (3) the cost of acquisition of an existing building. This basis includes the cost of the residential rental units and also facilities for use free and equally by all tenants and other facilities required by the project.

For example, if the total development costs of 100 residential units plus pool and other amenities is $4.5 million, of which $500,000 is for land, then the eligible basis would be $4.0 million in general. If 45 percent of the floor space (in residential units) but only 40 percent of the units are in low-income use, the qualified basis would be $1.6 million. If there is a charge for use of the pool or other facilities, the cost of these facilities would be excluded from the eligible basis.

There is a special provision to assure that low-income units are not inferior to other units in the project. The average construction or acquisition cost of low-income units must not be lower than the average for other units; if it is lower, the above average, non-low-income units will not be included in calculating the eligible basis. Similarly, rehabilitation expenditures may not be included in the eligible basis if such expenditures improve a unit beyond comparability with the low-income units.

The minimum set-aside is required to be met within twelve months after the building is placed in service. Qualifying units (and thus qualifying basis) can be added anytime thereafter if state credit authority is allocated to them. Additional qualifying basis receives only two-thirds of the initial credit rate, but it does so for the entire remaining compliance period (up to 14 years). If the additional credits are not allocated initially to the building and the credit provision has sunset, it appears that such additions to the qualifying basis will not be possible.

Qualifying Incomes

The tenant income ceiling for a unit to qualify as low-income depends on four items. First, area median income is determined under the same procedure as under the HUD Section 8 program. Second, 50 percent or 60 percent of the area median income, depending on whether the 20 percent or 40 percent minimum set-aside is being made, is calculated. Third, this amount is adjusted for family size in the same manner as under Section 8, i.e., with 10 percent less for each fewer person in family size below four. For family sizes of four or under, the applicable percentages of area median income are:

Family Size	50% Standard	60% Standard
4	50%	60%
3	45%	54%
2	40%	48%
1	35%	42%

Fourth, the special adjustments applied under the Section 8 program to areas of very low median income or very high housing costs are made. These adjustments do not incorporate consideration of the state median income.

The rent and income levels implied by these limits can be easily calculated for the nationwide median family income of about $28,000. For the household size of two, the maximum qualifying income would be $11,200 (i.e., 40% of $28,000) for the 20 percent set-aside at 50 percent of median income and $13,440 for the 40 percent set-aside at 60 percent of median income. The corresponding maximum gross rent levels (30 percent of monthly qualifying income) would be $280 and $336, respectively. These low income and rent levels reflect the tight targeting of this subsidy to households with very low incomes.

The determination of qualifying income is made on a continuing basis. Each year, the incomes of tenants in the qualifying units must be certified and compared with the income ceilings for that year for that family size. Tenants qualifying when initially occupying a rental unit will be considered to continue to qualify provided that their incomes do not exceed the maximum qualifying income by more than 40 percent. Some special rules apply to projects that satisfy a stricter set-aside requirement and that significantly restrict the rents on the low-income units relative to the other residential units.

Federally Assisted Projects

In general, new construction of federally subsidized projects is not eligible for the 9 percent credit. Instead, such construction or the acquisition of existing federally assisted projects is eligible for a 4 percent credit. Rehabilitation of existing projects is eligible for the 9 percent credit if the rehabilitation expenditures are not federally subsidized. However, it must be emphasized that, normally, existing projects are not eligible if they were built or have had a change of ownership within the preceding 10 years and that only those units in the projects that meet the income restrictions of the credit program can qualify. Exceptions can be made by the Secretary of the Treasury, in consultation with the Secretaries of HUD or Agriculture, as appropriate, for troubled projects or certain special cases.

Federal assistance seems to be fairly narrowly defined to include only tax-exempt financing or a below-market direct or indirect federal loan. The definition does not include Section 8 in general as a subsidy, including Section 8 Moderate Rehabilitation. The law specifically permits projects to receive 9 percent credits even though they benefit from federal grants, including those under the Community Development Block Grant, the Urban Development Action Grant, the Rental Rehabilitation Grant, and the Housing Development Grant programs, as long as the amount of the grant is excluded from the eligible basis.* The law also leaves the door open to state or local support.

Investor Limitations

Low-income projects generally are subject to the same limitation on passive losses as other rental real estate. However, two important exceptions are made. The $25,000 "active participant" exception from the loss limitation (see Chapter 3) is available to limited partners as well as "active participants" for purposes of the credit (i.e., thus permitting use of up to $7,000 in credits without any passive income). Second, this exception phases out at incomes between $200,000 and $250,000, rather than the $100,000 and $150,000 for most rental real estate. Unused credits can be applied against gain at time of sale, but any credits remaining would be lost.

This exception does not solve all of the problems posed by the anti-tax shelter provisions of the new law. For example, a large project primarily occupied by qualifying tenants will generate large amounts of both credits and passive losses over a long period. The ability of an individual investor to use both the credits and the passive losses will depend ultimately on the presence of significant amounts of "passive income" (see Chapter 3). Even so, few individual investors can be so

---

This last provision suggests that it is preferable to have federal grants to a rehabilitation project ascribed to the acquisition costs (which get the 4 percent credit) instead of to rehabilitation expenditures (which can get the 9 percent credit).

confident of their income and tax status over a 10 year period that this prospective stream of benefits will be valued fully. In addition, credit projects usually will require large continuing cash infusions because of the restricted rents, posing difficult practical problems for the usual limited partnership arrangements. For all of these reasons, it may be difficult to secure individual investors for credit projects.

An important alternative is C corporations, especially since they are exempt from the passive loss limitation. For example, a feasible procedure for using the credits for new construction may be to have a non-profit sponsor draw upon state or local subsidies and the credit to build low-income units, with the credits and losses being syndicated to a group of major corporations. The presence of the non-profit group could both facilitate getting the credits and add to the public relations aspects of the corporate involvement.

Recapture and Compliance

The credit is received annually for a period of ten years after the project is placed in service, but the project must meet continuously for 15 years the proportion of qualified basis in low-income use that determines its initial allocation of credits. It must first be in compliance no later than 12 months after it is placed in service. As noted above, incomes must be recertified annually. If a project falls out of compliance, the next available unit of comparable or smaller size must be occupied by a qualifying tenant.

If the project fails to rectify the non-compliance, the "accelerated portion" of the credit is subject to recapture. The "acceleration" refers to the fact that the credit is received over 10 years but is in return for keeping a portion of the project in qualifying use over a 15 year period. Thus one-third of the credit received under the initial allocation is received "early" and is subject to recapture during the first 10 years, with interest. This portion is phased-out over the last 5 years.

If the minimum set-aside (i.e., 20 percent or 40 percent) continues to be met, the recapture applies only to the portion of the basis that has fallen out of compliance. If the minimum is no longer met, all credits become subject to the recapture provision. If non-compliance is only with respect to the portions of the basis receiving additional credits over and above the initial allocation there is no recapture. This is because there is no accelerated portion of such credits.

The sale of the building also causes recapture. However, this recapture can be avoided if (1) the project has completed the 15 year compliance period or (2) bond for a "sufficient" amount is posted with the Treasury by the seller. In any case, the new owner would be allowed to receive any remaining credits, using the same qualified basis and credit percentage as the previous owner.

Other Provisions

Another notable facet of the program is that there appears to be no statutory limit on the size of a project qualifying for the credit. Thus a single family house or one building in a garden apartment project may qualify. However, a building with four or fewer units will not qualify if a unit is occupied by the owner or related person. Of course, the state credit authority may choose not to grant credits to any particular project. In any case, the administrative complexities of utilizing the credits will require some economies of scale.

Certain types of housing will not qualify for the credit, including nursing homes, sanitariums, lifecare facilities, retirement homes, hospitals, or trailer parks. On the other hand, the rental residential portions of mixed use developments can qualify.

As noted above, the gross rents on the qualifying units must be limited to 30 percent of the maximum qualifying income for the family size residing in the unit. This amount must include an allowance for tenant-paid utility costs. This rent ceiling is only what is charged to the tenant and may be net of federal or other rent subsidies. For example, payments under the Section 8 program would be excluded.

Finally, there are a number of annual reporting requirements to be met under the credit, both for the owner of the project and for the state credit allocation authorities.

ECONOMICS OF THE LOW-INCOME HOUSING CREDIT

The new credit will clearly be much more complicated to utilize than the tax incentives available under previous law. However, similar complexity has been present in all direct federal assistance programs and even in the tax-exempt bond program, yet these programs have been widely utilized. Presumably, experience and regulations will ease the difficulties. That still leaves the question of where and when the credit will be most worthwhile.

A simple calculation will show that the credit provides a significant incentive. If the total cost of development of a low-income unit is $45,000, of which $40,000 is the depreciable basis and thus eligible for the credit, a credit amount of 9 percent is $3,600 per year or $300 per month, on an after-tax basis. An after-tax benefit of $300 is equivalent to $417 in before-tax rent at the 28 percent tax rate. When compared with the rent of about $520 required for feasibility for such a project under the new law, it would appear that rents as low as $100 could be charged. Such rents would be well under the rent limits for the credit in all parts of the country.

Unfortunately, the financial mathematics are not quite that simple. In addition, there are important investor and market problems to be faced.

First, the amount of the credit will stay the same for 10 years, while the dollar value of the gap between the market rents required to make the project feasible without the credit and the permitted rents (i.e., the cost of using the credit) will expand with inflation. These future discrepancies between the amounts of the credit and the foregone rent income must be discounted to the present and translated into a measure of the effective amount of the credit.*

Second, the credit is paid over ten years, but the set-aside and rent requirements must be met for 15 years. Thus, there will be five years over which rents must remain below market but no further credits are received. However, these five years are far enough in the future that their influence is heavily discounted.

These two considerations imply that investors are not willing to offer a rent reduction equivalent to a 9 percent credit. Instead, we must calculate the present value equivalent of a 9 percent credit received over 10 years, in terms of a rent reduction over 15 years. The result is about a 7 percent credit (discounted at a 13 percent internal rate of return). Thus, in the example above, a discount of up to $324 in monthly rent could be offered, implying a rent of about $200 a month.** Such a rent would be under the rent limits for a two-person household in areas with median incomes at or above the $17,000-$20,000 range.

Despite the depth of the subsidy, it appears that the credit may be effective only for certain types of projects, depending on the appreciation potential or the presence of other subsidies. The discussion below of various different uses illustrates the issues involved. The judgments are based on analyses of possible projects using the credit done with the NAHB rental simulation model. This model is similar to models used by real estate investors and academics for project analysis. Key assumptions used for this analysis include a required after-tax internal rate of return of 13 percent, a 75 percent loan-to-value ratio, expected inflation of 5 percent, expected increases in rents of 3.5 percent, and a holding period of 15 years (and thus no recapture of credits at time of sale).

It could be argued that the credit should be discounted at a much lower rate than the rent differential, because the credit is guaranteed while rental incomes are uncertain. However, there are serious risks and uncertainties about the value of future credits. An individual investor may not owe sufficient tax, or may have too high an income or insufficient passive income, or be subject to the alternative minimum tax (against which the credit cannot be taken), any one of which situations would prevent him or her from currently using the credit. Moreover, there are risks of future changes in the tax law or recapture upon noncompliance or sale. All of these considerations suggest that the discount rate to be applied to the credit should include a risk premium similar to that of rental income.

**The rent discount is found by taking 7 percent of $40,000, dividing that amount by the after-tax value of a dollar of before-tax income ($.72) and finally dividing by 12 to put it on a monthly basis.*

100 Percent Low-Income Project

The 9 percent credit is intended to generate new construction or significant ($2,000 or more) rehabilitation of units for low-income households. Application of the credit to the NAHB simulation model of a typical middle-income new construction project, without changing any assumptions, suggests that rent levels permitted under the credits could be met (as indicated in the example above). However, there are also several good reasons to expect that such projects will not be feasible without additional, non-federal subsidies.

The major market problem confronting the credit in this case is the usual uncertainty about the market value of subsidized housing at time of resale. If the construction of such housing today is feasible only with direct or indirect subsidies, the future appreciation is likely to be significantly less than that of a market-rate project. In fact, there may be no equity value at all. Unless the project is built in an area capable of supporting it without the credit, the value in 15 years will depend heavily on future tax law, subsidy programs, and the luck of the market trends at the project's location over the period. Absence of an appreciation potential makes the financial feasibility of a 9 percent credit project marginal.

Such a project would also run large, continuing cash deficits and even larger tax losses. The cash deficits are probably less than the flow of credits, so that the investors might be willing to meet these cash needs out of their tax savings. However, the challenge of obtaining individual investors capable of taking both the large amounts of credits and the enormous tax losses seems nearly insurmountable. Finding a conventional source of financing for the project would be equally difficult. In the case of both an inability to use all credits and/or losses, and in the absence of significant appreciation potential, such projects do not appear to make economic sense without additional subsidy.

On the other hand, there may be significant feasibility for moderate amounts of rehabilitation to existing buildings in stable or rising low- and moderate-income areas. If the buildings are priced to offer reasonable returns under current market conditions, and rents are at or under the prescribed rent limits, then upgrading the property through the credit may be very attractive.

Both of these uses become more feasible if a state or local agency provides guarantees, interest subsidies, or other support. In general, while the 9 percent credit may not get many projects built by itself, it could provide significant impetus to public-private partnerships and state and local housing initiatives, as long as they do not include federally subsidized financing. Such efforts would also benefit from involvement of a regular corporation capable of utilizing all of the credits and the losses.

An interesting aspect of the 9 percent credit is that variation in depreciable development costs per unit (as opposed to land costs) have relatively little effect on the feasibility of the project. This small impact of quality upgrading or higher construction costs reflects the combined offset of increased credits, increased depreciation and an assumption of full market resale at the end of the 15 years (i.e., these factors fully compensate for higher construction costs). One result is that capital expenditures that can reduce maintenance and operating costs (which do not benefit from any subsidy) are highly attractive.

Tax-Exempt Financed Projects

The credit is available to tax-exempt financed projects. While tax-exempt financing by itself is still available, the new income restrictions make it unlikely that such projects will be feasible without also taking the credit. Since the only additional condition that must be met to receive and use a 4 percent credit is the acceptance of rent limits on the low-income units, it seems likely that users of tax-exempt financing will also utilize the credit generally in the future.

The 4 percent credit appears to provide the means for meeting the income and rent limits, assuming (1) that the 20 percent set-aside at 50 percent of median income is chosen, (2) that the entire project is expected to appreciate to the same degree as an all-market-rate project and (3) that the market-rate units are feasible in their own right under the new law. The first assumption is reasonable because the 20 percent set-aside concentrates benefits of the tax-exemption (assumed to be a 1.5 percent lower interest rate) on the fewest number of units. The second assumption of normal appreciation should also be reasonable if there are few physical and market differences between this and a 100 percent-market-rate project. The third assumption, that the market rent levels have already risen to meet the post-Tax Act required rents, is currently unrealistic. Thus, while the 4 percent credit may make multifamily tax-exempt financing attractive once more in the future, its widespread use probably depends on market rents rising from current levels (see Chapter 2).

One basic question related to tax-exempt financing is whether using tax-exempt financing plus the 4 percent credit on the set-aside portion is more attractive than using conventional financing and the 9 percent credit on the set-aside portion. Relatedly, is it more attractive (1) to finance both the acquisition cost and the rehab cost with tax-exempts and apply a 4 percent credit to the set-aside units or (2) to finance only the acquisition cost and seek a 9 percent credit on the qualified rehabilitation expenditures?

The answer mostly depends on the proportion of the project to be set aside for low-income occupancy. If the set-aside is not much more than 20 percent, it appears that tax-exempt financing plus the 4 percent credit provides about as much subsidy as the 9 percent credit. When considerations such as improved cash flow and reduced passive losses are taken into account, tax-exempt financing becomes more favorable (assuming that the issuance authority is obtainable). However, if 40 percent or more of the project might qualify for the credit, then the amount of credits becomes much greater and the rent ceilings become higher (because the income limit rises to 60 percent of median), so the 9 percent credit approach would normally be preferred.

FmHA Section 515 Projects

One of the first candidates for the new credits will be Farmers Home Administration Section 515 projects in the development pipeline.* These projects

---

It should be noted that projects begun before March 1, 1986 may be eligible for old law depreciation upon completion. If so, the credit can be taken only if the old law depreciation is given up. Such an election is likely to be desirable since the lower tax rates and passive loss limitations have reduced the value of rapid depreciation.

receive interest subsidies, but also require significant tax benefits for feasibility because of severe limitations on rents and cash distributions. They will be eligible to seek a 4 percent credit if placed into service in 1987. How will this credit compare with prior law tax benefits?*

It appears that the 4 percent credit plus whatever remaining depreciation benefits there are has an approximately similar present value as the prior-law tax benefits. The conclusion is reached under the assumption of a 13 percent after-tax discount rate and the assumption that the project would have been sold every 8 years under prior law in order to reestablish the tax benefits. On the other hand, Section 515 developers will still face some new difficulties related to finding investors able to use the credits and not affected by the limitation on passive losses. In addition, the income limits are lower for the credit than under the general programs. Most importantly, developers will have to secure allocations of the credit from the state credit authority. If all FmHA projects authorized for FY 1987 receive 4 percent credits, this use alone could require about 20 percent of the total credit authority.

Existing Assisted Projects

Just as new Section 515 projects depend upon tax benefits because of limits on cash returns, so do many existing federally assisted projects rely on tax benefits for providing market value. Tax benefits under prior law provided significant value to these projects, prompting extensive investment in them the last few years. The 4 percent credit appears to provide an equal undergirding of tax benefits. However, there are two major differences. First, as noted above, the tax benefits will be much more difficult to fully utilize under the new restrictions on tax shelters. Second, receipt of the credit is far from automatic. There may be an actual bias against granting credits to these projects, because the states have little stake in maintaining the value or preventing default among federally assisted projects.

The credit may also become embroiled in the issue of federally assisted projects being withdrawn from the federal programs under various owner options. Allocations of credits under the new law can be useful tools to keep projects in low-income use and thus the allocation process may become caught up in the controversies that frequently arise as a project owner considers dropping the project from a federal program.

---

* Prior law tax benefits such as rapid depreciation, if carried over into new law, would have been worth much less because of the lower tax rate and the end of the capital gains differential. The analysis here compares the value of those benefits under prior law tax rates with the value of the credit plus depreciation allowed under the new law at the new-law tax rates.

CONCLUSION

The low-income rental housing credit should be a significant new financing tool for low- and moderate-income housing. Clearly, it will take creativity and persistence to bring it to its full potential, but the effort should be worthwhile over the long-run. The political background suggests that the credit will be renewed and possibly improved before it expires. In fact, Congressional backers of the credit have indicated that they will seek whatever changes are needed to make it work.

Chapter 7

COMMERCIAL REAL ESTATE AND HISTORIC REHABILITATION

Michael S. Carliner
Staff Vice President, Economics and Housing Policy
National Association of Home Builders

The tax incentives for investment in commercial real estate will be sharply reduced under the new tax law. Depreciation will be stretched out, the preferential treatment of capital gains will be eliminated, and rehabilitation tax credits will be reduced. In addition, there will be restrictions on the use of losses from real estate investments to offset income from other business activities, portfolio income, or wage and salary income.

Exhibit 7.1 shows the relevant provisions under prior (1986) law and under the provisions of the Tax Reform Act of 1986, which governs tax liability beginning in 1987. The transition rules under which the provisions of the new law are phased in are complex and also deserve careful scrutiny (see the Appendix).

Exhibit 7.1
Major Provisions Affecting Commercial Real Estate

	Prior Law	1986 Reform Act (when fully effective)		Prior Law	1986 Reform Act (when fully effective)
Depreciation	19 yr., Straight Line usually used due to stringent recapture	31.5 yr. Straight Line	At-Risk Exemption	Yes	Only for third-party financing
Capital Gains	60% Exclusion (20% max. rate)	No Exclusion (28% max. rate)	Historic Rehab Tax Credit	25% with 1/2 basis adjustment	20% with full basis adjustment
Depreciation subject to Recapture	All depreciation unless straight-line was used	Not applicable (No cap. gains exclusion)	Nonhistoric Rehab Tax Credit	15% or 20% depending on age of building	10% for buildings built before 1936
Passive Loss Limitation	None	Rental losses only deductible against rental or passive income (5 year phase-in); except $25,000 in losses or $7,000 in credits allowed if "active" participant. Does not apply to investors in hotels who qualify as "material" participants.	Maximum Personal Tax Rate	50%	28% (effectively 33%)
			Alternative Minimum Tax Rate	20%	21%
			Real Estate-Related Preference Items for Minimum Tax	Depreciation in excess of straight line Capital Gains Exclusion	Depreciation in excess of 40 years straight line All "passive activity" losses (during phase-in) Interest on private purpose tax-exempt bonds Gain deferred by installment sale

MAJOR PROVISIONS AFFECTING COMMERCIAL REAL ESTATE

Depreciation

The recovery period for nonresidential structures has been extended from 19 years to 31.5 years, and depreciation expense must be calculated on a straight-line basis. In general the new schedule applies to property placed in service after December 31, 1986. However, if a binding contract was in effect or substantial construction (5 percent or $1 million) had occurred by March 31, 1986, the 19-year schedule will apply even if the structure is placed in service after 1986.

In the case of nonresidential property which is financed with tax-exempt bonds, the portion of the property attributable to such financing must be depreciated over 40 years.

Capital Gains

One of the attractions of investment in commercial real estate has been the fact that gains on sale of the property have been taxed at preferential capital gains rates. If the property has been depreciated using the straight line method, the accumulated depreciation and any appreciation above original cost have been subject to taxation at the reduced rate.

The new law eliminates the preferential treatment of capital gains. For gains realized in 1987, the maximum individual rate on capital gains will be 28 percent, even though ordinary income will be subject to higher rates in that transition year. But beginning in 1988, capital gains will be taxed at the same rate as ordinary income.

As under prior law, increases in property values will not be taxed until the gain is realized through sale. The higher tax rate on gains from sale may encourage owners to hold on to properties longer.

Under prior law, many tax strategies were centered around having income treated as capital gains, rather than ordinary income. With the rate differential removed, this is no longer a consideration. One aspect of prior law where this was particularly important was a provision that said that if a nonresidential building was depreciated using the accelerated 175 percent declining-balance method, any accumulated depreciation was subject to "recapture"--taxation at ordinary income rates--upon sale. If the straight line method of depreciation was used, however, the entire difference between the sales price and the depreciated basis was subject to capital gains treatment. The result of that rule was to cause most nonresidential rental property to be depreciated using the straight line method. Of course, the new law provides only straight-line depreciation. However, with the rate differential eliminated, it may be more attractive to choose accelerated declining- balance depreciation where it is still available. Thus, for property placed in service in 1986 or subject to a binding contract on March 1, 1986, it should be possible to calculate depreciation on a 19-year 175 percent declining-balance basis, and generally it will be attractive to do so, unless one thinks that the capital gains differential will be reinstated.

Limits on Losses

As with rental housing, there would be new limits on the use by individuals of losses from commercial property to offset income from wages and salaries, portfolio income, or income from "active" trade or business. Aside from a limited exception for small "mom and pop" active owners of rental properties, all rental activities would be considered "passive," even for general partners and sole proprietors who materially participate in management of the property.

The limit on use of passive losses to offset other income is generally applicable only to individuals and subchapter S corporations. Moreover, it is subject to a gradual phase-in on existing investments. However, the losses on passive investments allowed under the phase-in will be treated as preference items under the minimum tax for individuals.

For hotels and other real property that is rented on a day-to-day basis, special rules apply. Unlike other rental activities, which are automatically defined to be passive, hotels can be considered as active businesses, even for high income individual taxpayers, if the taxpayer materially participates in management. This is because a hotel is assumed to provide a broad package of services, rather than simply use of the asset. However, material participation is not an easy standard to meet. It requires involvement on a regular, continuous, and substantial basis. It is a much stricter standard than the active participation required under the "mom and pop landlord" exception. However, several commentators have suggested that investors in condominium hotels could qualify as material participants.

Precisely how far this exception can be taken is not clear. For example, congregate housing also involves a large service component, but not the short-term rental aspect characteristic of hotels. Further guidance is awaited in this area.

REHABILITATION TAX CREDITS

The new tax law retains the credit for rehabilitation of old or historic structures, but the size of the credit is reduced. Moreover, for historic structures the full amount of the credit must be subtracted from the depreciable basis, and non-historic structures are only eligible for credit if they were originally placed in service before 1936. There have also been changes made to the "external walls" requirement.

The credit for rehabilitation of certified residential and nonresidential historic structures will be 20 percent, down from 25 percent. For nonhistoric nonresidential structures built before 1936, a 10 percent rehabilitation credit will be available. That will replace the 15 percent and 20 percent credits available under prior law.

The new, reduced, credits will apply to property placed in service after December 31, 1986. There is a grandfather clause for projects being completed under contracts binding on March 1, 1986 and put into service before 1994.

Credits will be subject to passive/rental loss rules and similar restrictions, except that a special exception allows taxpayers with non-passive income of under $200,000 to use credits equivalent to a loss of $25,000 (i.e., $7,000 credit in the 28 percent bracket) to offset tax liability from other income, whether or not they are active participants. This exception is phased out for taxpayers with total non-passive incomes between $200,000 and $250,000, i.e., higher than the phase-out range for the $25,000 active participant exception.

Because of the up-front nature of the credit, this exception is of limited value. It will require parcelling out the equity in a rehabilitation project to a large number of small investors. Alternatively, individuals with sufficient passive income to take advantage of the credits could become investors, but in that case as well the lump-sum nature of the credit would make it difficult to use. Credits that cannot be used in one year could be carried forward, and used against passive income or the special exception in later years, but unlike passive losses, unused credits cannot be used in full upon disposition of the investment.

Corporations are generally not restricted from offsetting other income with passive losses and credits, such as the rehabilitation tax credit. Thus, corporations may become more important sources of equity investment in rehabilitations.

The reductions in the credits and the limitations on use of credits will probably reduce the values of existing structures that would be candidates for rehabilitation. Buildings that are more than thirty years old but have been built since 1936 will be particularly affected, since they will no longer be eligible for credits at all. In addition, the relative attractiveness of rehabilitation compared to new construction would be reduced, since the reduction in the tax credit is equivalent to an increase in development costs.

OTHER ASPECTS

There are a number of other aspects concerning the Tax Act and commercial real estate that should be noted. One aspect is the change in depreciation for personal property included in a project. Another is the new requirement that leasehold improvements be depreciated over the appropriate ACRS life without regard to the lease term. Similarly, lease acquisition costs must be amortized not only over the term of the lease, but also beyond, over the term of any reasonably anticipated renewals.

There may be some steps that commercial property owners can take to minimize the impact of the passive loss limitation. One that has been suggested is to give long-term tenants some equity interest or renewable fixed-rent leases in return for higher current rents. In any case, it appears that giving tenants in weak markets free rent over the early portion of their leases will be significantly more expensive to landlords when the losses cannot be currently deducted.

Chapter 8

SECOND HOMES, RESORT PROPERTY AND LAND DEVELOPMENT

Daniel N. Chambers
Housing Policy Analyst
National Association of Home Builders

SECOND HOMES AND RESORT PROPERTY

The market for second homes and resort property is a combination of several narrower markets. Some second homes are intended to be available full-time for the use of the owner. Others are simply a rental investment property. Still others are purchased for both the pleasure of partial personal use and for the business of rental use. The impact of the Tax Reform Act on the market for second homes is the composite of the reactions of each of these types of buyers to the provisions that specifically affect them. We examine each separately.

Second-Home Usage and Tax Treatment

Second-home owners choose how many days per year to either rent out a second home or use it personally. This choice will determine whether the home is considered a personal residence or a rental property for tax purposes. If someone occupies their second home for more than 14 days, or 10 percent of rental use, whichever is higher, then the second home is considered to be primarily a personal residence and is accorded tax treatment similar to that of the primary residence, with mortgage interest and property taxes generally deductible. If it is rented out as well for more than 14 days, some additional deductions for rental operating expenses are allowed (and the rental income must be reported). The home is not considered a second residence if the owner's personal use is 14 days or less (or 10 percent of rental usage or less); then it is treated the same as any other rental property.

Second Homes As Personal Residences

As a personal residence, the second home retains full deductibility of property taxes. Interest on mortgages secured by the second residence also remains deductible according to the same rule applying to the principal residence. As described in Chapter 1, interest on any debt against the second home which is outstanding on August 16, 1986 is deductible in full (as long as it does not exceed fair market value). For debt secured after that date, the interest is deductible only for debt up to the original purchase price of the second home plus the cost of improvements, or if the loan is used for qualified medical or educational expenses.

Of course, the deduction of interest and property taxes will generate lower tax savings than under prior law, because of the lower tax rates. This effect is greatest at the higher income levels, levels which are relatively more common among buyers in the second-home market than in the market for primary residences. Moreover, the decision to buy a second home is probably more sensitive to its after-tax cost than is the choice of how much to spend on a primary residence. Thus this market has been and may continue to be more heavily affected by the prospective drop in tax rates.

The new restriction on mortgage interest deductibility probably applies to each residence separately. While this interpretation may be changed by Treasury regulations, it appears currently that homeowners will generally not be able to refinance their primary residence beyond its cost as a method of purchasing a second residence, and still deduct the interest without limit. Such an interpretation of the new rule may make it difficult for some buyers to provide the downpayment needed to purchase a second home.

Interest on debt secured to buy time-sharing weeks remains deductible, since up to six weeks of time-sharing arrangements are treated as a single residence. Interest on debt against any third or fourth home will no longer be deductible, so taxpayers with more than two residences, including time-sharing, must decide on which of their other residences to treat as their second home for tax purposes.

Second Homes As Rental Properties

For taxpayers who limit their use of their second home to no more than 14 days or 10 percent of total use, the property is treated for tax purposes as any other rental property, meaning (in general) that the owner reports gross rental income and is allowed to deduct utilities, maintenance, depreciation, property taxes, and mortgage interest as business expenses. Under prior law, tax losses generated by a rental second home could offset any other type of income, including wages or salaries. But under the Act, all rental activities are subject to the passive loss limitation, which allows rental losses to offset only income from other rental (or passive) activities. (See Chapter 3 for a full discussion of this limitation.)

However, there is a special provision in the Act which will likely apply to most second-home owners and will permit up to $25,000 per year in net passive losses to be used against any other type of income. This special provision applies to passive losses for "active participants" with adjusted gross incomes below $100,000 (the $25,000 allowance is phased out between $100,000 and $150,000 income). Owners of rental second homes are active participants as long as they retain decision-making authority such as the setting of rents and approval of repairs, even if they turn over the daily management of the unit to someone else. Most second-home owners make these decisions and many will also meet the income restriction; hence, the passive loss limitation is not expected to affect most of the second-home market.

Personal Residences Which Are Also Rented Out

Some households own a second home which both qualifies as a second residence and is rented out for part of the year as well. In this case, the owner can deduct annual mortgage interest and property taxes in full without regard to the passive loss limitation. In addition, operating expenses (depreciation, maintenance and utilities) incurred during the rental period are deductible subject to some limitations. Under both prior law and the Act the main restriction is that a second residence cannot generate tax losses for the owner: deductions for operating expenses can only offset rental income generated from the second home, not other sources of income (including, under the Act, net income from other passive activities). Excess, unused deductions (other than for interest and taxes) in any year are lost, i.e., they are not carried forward to offset net rental income from the second home in future years.

To find the allowable deductions for these other rental expenses, the taxpayer first calculates the percentage of rental usage out of total usage (rental plus personal usage); then, this percentage is applied to each annual expense to attribute it to rental usage. The owner attributes mortgage interest and property taxes to rental usage, too, even though the deductibility of these is not strictly related to how many days the property is rented. Gross rental income less the attributed interest and taxes is the limit for deducting the attributed expenses for depreciation, maintenance and utilities.*

Installment Sales of Resort Property

The installment sales method of reporting profit on housing sales is severely restricted under the Act. As discussed in Chapter 9, this restriction takes the form of a proportionate disallowance of the amount of profit which can be reported in years following the sale year. The Act, however, allows the unrestricted installment method to be used by dealers of time-shares or unimproved land (as long as neither the dealer nor an associate develops the land). In either instance, the dealer can use the installment sales method of reporting profits, but must pay interest to the government (at 100 percent of the Applicable Federal Rate for the maturity of the installment note) on the deferral of tax liability attributable to the installment use. Also, the dealer cannot use the installment method on more than six weeks of time-share sold to any taxpayer and his or her immediate family.

---

* If an owner has been careful not to exceed the 14 day or 10 percent limit on personal use up to now in order to maintain full rental status for the house, he or she may now find it advantageous to extend their personal use. For a rental second home, if the owner cannot utilize the passive losses from the investment (because the owner's income is too high to qualify for the $25,000 exception and the owner has no net passive income), then total deductions are limited to gross rental income. In this case, deductions could be increased by establishing the house as a personal residence if the owner's rental operating expenses plus mortgage interest and property taxes attributable to rental use at least offset gross rental income.

Market Impact

The continued deductibility of mortgage interest and property taxes on the second home, including time-shares, is the best news for the second-home market. But the prospects of the Act's cut-backs in rental tax benefits and the reduced tax savings on personal use (resulting from the lower tax rates) are causing already some weakness in the market for second homes. Some of the wealthiest owners may scale back since their tax rates will fall sharply and interest on more than two homes is no longer deductible at all.

The largest impact will be on the market for second homes held mainly as rental properties. Since nearly half of all second homes held for vacation or occasional use by their owners are rented to others much of the time, the Act's adverse impact on rental housing in general (see Chapter 2) may substantially curtail second-home purchases. This, in turn, will cause a decline in the price of undeveloped resort land. Over time, the resort rental market will adjust through higher rental rates. However, the adjustment process will be slowed because vacationers, who have many more alternatives than do renters of year-round housing, may be resistant to higher rents.

LAND DEVELOPMENT

The effects of the Tax Act are so pervasive that there are even ramifications for land owning and development, as well as for housing construction itself. Three of the areas of impact are (1) investment land, (2) development land, and (3) installment sales of land.

The economics of holding raw land as a long-term investment are changed radically under the Tax Act. One of the major attractions of such an investment has been the low capital gains tax rate on long-term appreciation. When leveraged, i.e., when held subject to a mortgage, this advantage was magnified, since the carrying cost was deductible at ordinary tax rates (subject to the investment interest limitation) while the return was taxed at capital gains rates. The drop in the ordinary tax rate and the rise in the capital gains rate increase the carrying costs and reduce the return to holding speculative land and may cause declines in its price, relative to the price ultimately expected at time of development.

At some point, land held for long-term appreciation is developed. At that point, if the seller is characterized as a dealer, the capital gains are taxed at ordinary rates. This provision has led to efforts to avoid characterization as a dealer. However, as long as the capital gains tax differential is out of the tax code, attaining non-dealer status or selling to a dealer before subdividing land will not generally be so critical. Of course, there is a strong possibility that the rate differential may be reintroduced within several years.

Another provision affecting some land sales is the limitation on tax deferrals through installment sales. This provision is discussed at length in Chapter 9. However, there are two important special aspects of it with respect to land development. First, as noted above, dealers in "unimproved" land can utilize the full deferral of tax under the installment sales provision, at the price of paying interest on the deferred tax. Second, sales of <u>investment</u> land may be exempt from the new limitations. This possibility rests on the wording of the law, which applies the new rules to "casual sales exceeding $150,000 of real property (other than certain farm property) used in the seller's trade or business or held for the production of rental income." Since investment land is generally not used in a trade or business nor held for rental income, it may not be subject to the limitations. Moreover, there is a special exception for property used in a trade or business if that trade or business is farming, as is sometimes the case for speculatively held land.

Chapter 9

OTHER PROVISIONS RELEVANT TO REAL ESTATE

Floyd L. Williams
Tax Counsel, Government Affairs Division
National Association of Home Builders

The Tax Reform Act of 1986 contains several provisions, not discussed elsewhere, that will have an impact upon real estate. This chapter addresses installment sales, corporate property distributions, and selected accounting provisions.

INSTALLMENT SALES

Prior law generally required gain or loss from the sale of property to be recognized in the taxable year in which the property was sold. However, gain from certain sales of property in exchange for which the seller received deferred payments was reported under the installment method, unless the taxpayer-seller elected otherwise. In general, the installment method applied to dispositions of property where at least one payment was to be received after the close of the taxable year in which the disposition occurred.

Under the installment method of prior law, a taxpayer recognized annually only a proportionate amount of gain resulting from a disposition of property. Such amount was equal the amount of any payment received times the ratio of gross profit under the contract to the total contract price. If an installment obligation was disposed of, gain or loss was recognized equal to (1) the difference between the amount realized and the basis of the obligation in the case of satisfaction at other than face value, or sale or exchange of the obligation, or (2) the difference between the fair market value of the obligation at the time of disposition and the basis of the obligation in the case of any other disposition.

Under the installment sale method of accounting, taxes on profits could be deferred until a later time. Meanwhile, the entire outstanding amount of unrealized profits, including the portion to be paid in taxes, could be earning interest under the installment note. Such an approach has been commonly used in the sale of commercial and rental property, either for its intrinsic financial advantages or simply as a side effect of providing needed seller financing. The tax deferral available under the installment method was also a major advantage in the case of builder bond financing (see Chapter 5).

The new law reduces substantially the benefits of installment sale treatment on casual (i.e., non-dealer) sales of real property used in a trade or business or held for the production of income, if the sales price exceeds $150,000. The goal of the new law is to force recognition of gain to the extent that the deferral of the payments is directly or indirectly financed by the taxpayer through borrowings. In other words, only to the extent that a taxpayer carries the complete burden of foregoing immediate payment on a sale may the tax on the sale be fully deferred.

Generally, the installment sale benefit on obligations arising in this type of transaction (known as "applicable installment obligations") is reduced in proportion to the ratio of the taxpayer's total indebtedness to its total assets. The new law achieves this reduction in benefits by treating a portion of the amount owed on applicable installment obligations at the end of a year as if that portion had been paid on those obligations in that year. Subsequent actual payments on such obligations are free of tax to the extent of previous "deemed" payments. Deemed payments (known as "allocable installment indebtedness" or AII) are determined in accordance with the following formula:

AII = $\dfrac{\text{Average yearly indebtedness}}{\text{Face amount of all installment obligations + adjusted basis of other assets}}$ X Face amount of applicable installment obligations

For purposes of this computation, the taxpayer may elect to compute adjusted basis using straight-line depreciation over the depreciable lives used in computing earnings and profits. Indebtedness is defined very broadly for purposes of this computation. That is, it includes all accounts payable and accrued expenses, as well as the usual forms of debt. The amount that is determined to be a deemed payment under the above-described formula is multiplied by the gross profit ratio on the sale to determine the portion of the deemed payment that must be treated as taxable gain.

The effect of this "proportionate disallowance" rule may be illustrated by the following example. Assume a taxpayer sells investment property (e.g., resort property held for the production of rental income) on the installment method for $400,000, and that no payments are received in the year of sale. The aggregate adjusted basis of the taxpayer's other assets is $600,000 and his total indebtedness is $500,000. Under the new law, the taxpayer would treat $200,000 as a payment in the year of sale. That is,

$$\dfrac{\$500{,}000}{\$400{,}000 + \$600{,}000} \quad X \quad \$400{,}000 = \$200{,}000$$

The taxpayer then would apply his gross profit ratio for this sale to determine what portion of the $200,000 deemed payment is taxed as gain in the year of sale.

For affiliated groups, or groups of businesses under common control, deemed payments are computed for the group as a whole and then are allocated among the group members. In the case of an individual, the proportionate disallowance computation does not take into account certain farm property or personal use property (e.g., a principal residence), or indebtedness that is secured only by such property.

Dealer sales of unimproved lots or timeshares are not subject to the proportionate disalowance rules if the dealer elects to pay interest on the deferral of its tax liability attributable to use of the installment method. For purposes of this election, a parcel of land is not to be considered to have been improved or developed if it merely has been provided with the benefits of common infrastructure items, such as roads and sewers. In addition, a timeshare for this purpose is a right to use a specified parcel of residential real property for a period not exceeding six weeks per year.

The proportionate disallowance rule for non-dealer sales applies to sales after August 16, 1986, in taxable years ending after December 31, 1986.

CORPORATE DISTRIBUTIONS

The new law has significant implications for corporate mergers and acquisitions and for dispositions of real estate by large subchapter C corporations. Of major importance is the revision of rules for the taxation of liquidating distributions, which, in effect, repeals the long-standing General Utilities case. Under the General Utilities rule, a corporation generally did not recognize gain or loss on a liquidating distribution.

The new law provides that gains and losses must be recognized by the corporation on the distribution of property by a liquidating corporation as if the property were sold to the shareholders at its fair market value. In the case of property that is subject to a liability, or where a shareholder assumes a liability in connection with the liquidating distribution, the fair market value of the property will be treated as not less than the amount of the liability.

Similar to liquidating distributions, the new law provides that the distribution of appreciated property by a corporation as a dividend or in redemption of its stock will result in the recognition of gain by the corporation as if the property were sold to the corporation's shareholders at its fair market value. Most importantly, the net gain from disposition of assets by a corporation no longer will be exempt from corporate level tax despite liquidation of the corporation within 12 months of the disposition. Instead, all such gain will be taxed at the corporate level. Thus, C corporations holding appreciated property will no longer have a way to avoid double taxation of capital gains.

Another important provision of the new law taxes at the maximum corporate rate any gain recognized from the sale or distribution of property by a subchapter S corporation that was formerly a subchapter C corporation (i.e. regular corporation) during the ten-year period after its subchapter S status is effective. This rule applies whether or not the property is distributed to a shareholder. Subchapter S corporations that make a subchapter S election for tax years beginning before 1987 can avoid this 10-year period and avoid the double tax effect of the repeal of General Utilities.

In general, the new rules apply to liquidations completed after 1986. Thus, immediate action would be required in order to avoid the new rule. However, liquidations completed before 1988 are exempt from the new rules if completed pursuant to a plan adopted before August 1, 1986. Also, certain liquidations completed before 1988 are exempt if certain actions were taken before November 20, 1985. Most importantly, there is an exception to the general rule for certain smaller corporations. Corporations not exceeding $5 million in value that are more than 50 percent owned directly or indirectly by 10 or fewer "qualified persons" have until the end of 1988 to complete a liquidation, even if the liquidation was not planned before August 1, 1986. The exception is phased out for closely-held corporations with values between $5 and $10 million and does not apply in connection with ordinary income assets, short-term capital assets or installment obligations.

MISCELLANEOUS ACCOUNTING PROVISIONS

The new law makes significant changes in the area of accounting methods and periods. Provisions that will affect builders in particular, in addition to the installment sale method revision discussed above, deal with stricter capitalization rules for self-constructed assets and long-term contracts.

Under the new law, construction period interest must be capitalized and added to the basis of self-constructed real property. This rule applies to interest paid or incurred after December 31, 1986, with respect to assets where construction began after February 28, 1986.

The provisions applicable to long-term contracts, effective for contracts entered into after February 28, 1986, require businesses to use one of two special methods to account for such contracts: (1) a modified percentage of completion method, or (2) a "40-60 method" under which 40% of contract income is accounted for under a modified percentage-of-completion method and 60% is accounted for under another permissible method (e.g., cash, accrual, or completed contract method). However, small contractors that perform real property contracts lasting less than two years can use the present law completed contract method. For purposes of this exception, a small contractor is a business with three-year average annual gross receipts of $10 million or less.

Chapter 10

ADAPTING REAL ESTATE BUSINESSES TO THE TAX REFORM ACT OF 1986

Leonard Silverstein
Senior Partner
Silverstein & Mullens
Washington, D.C.

The Tax Reform Act of 1986--officially designated as The Internal Revenue Code of 1986--demands a prompt reevaluation of legal structures and business practices by all persons involved in real estate operations, including home building, and land development, and multifamily apartment, commercial and shopping center construction. Indeed, for most builders, the concerns discussed herein necessitate both a long range review and, for those who can adapt to change prior to the close of 1986, certain immediate short term adjustments as well. To identify many of the issues which must be confronted, consider the following hypothetical situation.

"THE HARRIS COMPANIES"

"Harris Homes" is the trade name of "The Harris Companies," a family business which commenced operation shortly after World War II. The founder, Joseph "Joe" Harris, started his career in the construction and sale of single family residences. Currently, he has two grown sons (Tom and Harry) in business with him, who have taken over the construction and sale of houses, while Joe has confined his work to the sale of lots to Tom and Harry and third persons. Much later in his career, Joe began the construction of apartment houses and several office buildings. While all of these are fully rented, they still generate tax losses (because of straight-line depreciation and interest). Joe also owns limited partnership interests in an office building partnership built by unrelated persons.

Joe also owns all of the stock of a "C" (i.e., not a Subchapter S) corporation which owns a highly profitable warehouse (built in 1979) which it rents to unrelated persons. The value of the warehouse and land on which it is situated well exceeds its depreciated cost.

Apart from their single family residence business, Tom and Harry also have underway an apartment house. They also are general partners in two office buildings in which Joe and several "outside investors" are limited partners. These office buildings still "throw off" tax losses as well as cash flow.

Because of the decline in interest rates in 1986, Joe has recently refinanced his personally owned apartments, and reinvested the proceeds in listed stocks and bonds, from which he receives substantial dividend income. Joe also holds several major pieces of land for long term gain, in addition to his "regular" inventory land for lot development.

The actual work of the Harris Companies is carried out by three Subchapter S Corporations: the Joseph Harris Company (which acquires land for lot development and resale); the TH Corporation (which provides services to The Harris Companies for lot improvement, but also constructs homes) and the HT Corporation (which manages and rents the apartments and sells the single family homes). Each of these companies is on a cash basis with November 30 fiscal years.

As Joe's age and wealth have increased his interest in "charities" has increased and he would like to make more and larger gifts to civic causes, his college and other educational organizations, such as the educational arm of NAHB.

Although Joe is delighted that the new law would in general reduce income tax rates, he also realizes (because of NAHB publications and meetings) that real estate has been a major "target" of the new bill. For this reason, a conference of The Harris Companies tax advisors is called.

GENERAL STRATEGIES

The tax advisors state that it will first be necessary for the Harris family to shift the focus of their real estate tax thinking because of the radical changes caused by the new tax law. For example, commencing in 1988, capital gains will no longer have substantial significance. Thus, profits from land sales, whether part of inventory land or long term investment land, will be taxed in the same manner as profits from the sale of homes. Further, the corporate tax rate will be 34 percent after 1987 (as compared to 46 percent in 1986) and will exceed the 28 percent tax rate on individuals. Accordingly, no longer will it be useful to utilize a "C" corporation, such as the Warehouse Corporation, to accumulate earnings at the corporate level in order to avoid a second and higher tax rate on dividends distributed to shareholders. The use of a Subchapter S corporation, such as the Joseph Harris Company, may become even more advantageous than under pre-1987 law since its use combines the benefit of a single tax on the Warehouse Corporation earnings with the lower (ultimately 28 percent) rate.

Other developments under the new law include severe restrictions imposed upon the offset of portfolio income (such as the dividends and interest which Joe receives from his refinancing) by losses, both for regular and minimum tax purposes. And, in a major change from long-standing provisions, liquidation of a C corporation (such as the Warehouse Corporation) will, after 1986, produce corporate level tax in addition to depreciation recapture (if any) on the excess of the value of corporate held property over its adjusted basis (see Chapter 9).

The tax advisors, of course, point out that the so-called "effective dates" of the new rules differ widely and each pertinent rule should be carefully examined to determine its precise implication in a specific case. Finally, the advisors also note that the tax rates are "blended" for 1987 so that individuals in the top bracket will be subject to a 38.5 percent ordinary rate (but 28 percent on capital gains) and corporations will be subject to a 40 percent rate with a 34 percent rate on capital gains.

PRE-1987 TAX PLANNING

Because of the delayed effective dates in certain areas, the tax advisors suggest that Joe, Tom and Harry consider certain possibilities.

Capital Gains on Investment Land and Buildings

The investment land held by Joe for long term yield may well qualify for capital gains treatment under present (1986) law. Even though Joe is effectively a "dealer" in land (with respect to land held for lot sales and development), authority exists under present law for separate treatment as a capital gain for land held for investment provided such holding is independent of the inventory land. Accordingly, the tax advisors suggest that Joe consider a 1986 disposition of the land. Whether or not this should, in fact, occur depends upon whether the savings of 8 points in capital gains treatment is more valuable than the loss (net of 20 percent tax in 1986 compared to 28 percent in 1987, plus state and local tax burden) of the benefits of future appreciation in value. The tax advisors also make clear to Joe that the question of whether the land qualifies for capital gains treatment remains a question of fact and that the risk of an adverse audit, if the land is sold in 1986, must also be taken into account. After 1987, when capital gains are scheduled to be treated as ordinary income, that issue, of course, disappears.*

Similar 20 percent capital gains possibilities exist with respect to Joe's apartment houses and office buildings. Since these have been depreciated on a straight line basis, there are no depreciation recapture concerns. Moreover, the major new so-called "passive loss" restrictions of the new law would appear, in the case of rental structures, to prevent the use of losses realized from the depreciation, mortgage interest payments, and other expenses attributable to the structures against the profits realized by Joe from lot sales (as now occurs under present law).**

If Joe holds property which has been sold on the installment basis, and has on hand unpaid installment notes, consideration can be given to realizing the deferred gain in 1986 at current 20 percent capital gains rates. This may be achieved by "disposing" of the installment obligations in 1986 (for example, by discounting them with the bank or other purchaser, or in limited cases by contributing them to charity). Absent such a transaction, it is not possible to "elect out" of installment treatment.

Also, the new proportionate disallowance rule concerning the installment sales method of reporting profits does not apply to dealers of unimproved lots, as long as the residential development is not done by a dealer or an affiliate. See Chapter 9 for more details on the installment sales method.

**Even though the passive loss limitation is "retroactive" in that it applies to losses generated for existing properties using the old, accelerated depreciation, there is a 5-year phase-in which allows for partial use of such losses. See Chapter 3 and the Appendix for more details.*

Once again, the tax advisors caution that "the tax tail should not wag the business dog." Accordingly, sales of land and othe property should be sought only if, in Joe's view, there is no opportunity for long term appreciation. The net after-tax benefits from the lower tax rates applicable to a 1986 transaction. Alternatively, if Tom and Harry will be in the position to utilize the passibe losses, it may be advantageous for Joe to sell a building to them before the end of 1986, thereby giving them 19 years depreciation treatment. For that matter, Joe may consider holding the buildings permanently and passing them to his wife or children with stepped-up basis equal to their value at date of Joe's death.

The Warehouse Corporation

The tax advisors point out that complex principles govern disposition of the warehouse (or the Warehouse Corporation shares). Joe can dispose of the warehouse at a net federal tax cost of 20 percent on the built-in profit, provided, during 1986, the following occurs: (1) a buyer can be found for the shares of the Warehouse Corporation and such shares are sold before 1987 (so that the buyer of the shares can himself liquidate the corporation before 1987); (2) a buyer can be found who will accept only the assets, so a so-called "Section 337 liquidation" plan can be executed (whereby the Warehouse Corporation sells all of its assets and completely liquidates before 1987); (3) even if a buyer cannot be found, the Warehouse property can be distributed to Joe as the sole shareholder during 1986 and sold in 1987. Otherwise, the taxable gains upon disposition of the warehouse will, after 1986, be taxed at the corporate level as well as the personal.

As a preliminary consideration to the disposition to the property in any of the above described cases, review must be made of the "collapsible corporation" status of the Warehouse Corporation. Because the building was completed in 1979 and is therefore more than 3 years old, it is very probable that the collapsible corporation rules (which would tax the gain at 50 percent instead of 20 percent) will not apply. On the other hand, for example, if very major improvements had been effected within the preceding three years so that the warehouse could be considered a newly constructed property, a collapsible corporation danger might exist.*

---

* Whether or not a corporation is "collapsible" presents difficult questions. For example, the mere fact that the Warehouse Corporation has been in existence for many years does not necessarily preclude collapsible corporation characterization, causing gain on transaction to be taxed at a Federal rate of 50 percent rather than 20 percent. But important exceptions to the general rule of collapsibility provide, depending on the facts, substantial certainty that the collapsible tax will be avoided. Thus, to the extent that more than 3 years have passed since "completion" of construction of the warehouse, the interim collapsible tax does not apply. Unfortunately, however, renovations if substantial can be regarded as the commencement of new construction within 3 years, thus precluding the application of the three year rule. If the Warehouse Corporation held several separate properties-- for example, warehouses located in different parts of the metropolitan area-- collapsible characterization can be avoided if 30 percent or more of the gain realized on the liquidation is attributable to a property (e.g., a very old warehouse) with respect to which it can be determined that two-thirds of the income to be derived from the property has already been realized, or a purchased warehouse held by the corporation (without substantial renovation) for more than three years.

If a collapsible corporation danger exists and the risk of ordinary income treatment is sufficiently serious, consideration should be given to holding the property in C corporation status permanently or, alternately, to liquidating it after 1986, preferably in 1988 or later when ordinary income treatment would be limited to 28 percent. In this latter case, however, corporate capital gains tax of 34 percent will first be payable with respect to the corporation's gain in the warehouse property. At last, a possible very attractive alternative would be to elect Sub S status for the coporation before the end of 1986. If the timing of the corporation's fiscal year permits such an election in November or December of 1986, Joe will be able to dispose of the warehouse and dissolve the corporation without paying corporate-level tax at any time later than three years after the conversion. (See Chapter 9 for a discussion of the provisions for corporations regarding the recognition of gain or loss on liquidating sales and distributions of property.)

At-Risk Rules

Commencing in 1987 the so-called "at risk" rules apply in modified form to real estate transactions. Henceforth, in the construction or acquisition of an office building, apartment house or shopping center, Tom and Harry can receive the benefit of borrowed funds as part of their depreciable basis only if the mortgage or other loan is made from an unrelated financial institution (such as a savings and loan association) or, if financed by a related party, if the terms of the loan are at reasonable, commercial rates (thus ruling out an "equity kicker" or other similar participatory arrangement). Accordingly, after 1986, it will no longer be possible to borrow from a relative or a business entity in which the borrower has an interest. For this reason, if financial arrangements for Tom and Harry's new structures involve related commercial lenders and "kickers" or if they decide to buy one of Joe's buildings with his providing the financing, these should be completed before 1987 to avoid the new at-risk rules as well as to secure better depreciation. (Chapter 3 contains a discussion of the at-risk rules.)

Charitable Contribution of Land

In light of Joe's heightened interest in charitable causes, the tax advisors recommend that he consider a possible "last chance" opportunity to deduct the full value of land without causing (as will occur after 1986) any addition to his minimum tax base. Under present law, Joe is in a position in 1986 to obtain a deduction for the charitable contribution to the extent that the value of the land does not exceed 30 percent of his income for the year. Assuming that some portion of Joe's income is in a top marginal bracket of 50 percent, he will realize approximately 55 percent of the value of the land (taking into account state and local taxes) in income tax savings. In contrast, were Joe to sell the land, the net after tax proceeds would approximate 75 percent of the value of the land. Thus, Joe can benefit the charity of his choice at an approximate cost of 20 cents per dollar. Moreover, under limited circumstances similar arrangements can be made with his private foundation, if he has one or can form one effectively before the close of 1986. Accordingly, the year 1986 represents an ideal year to make large charitable gifts, either through "banking" them in a private foundation or in a public charity in order to receive the full benefit of the 50 percent deduction and avoidance of minimum tax.

POST-1986 CONSIDERATIONS

The Harris family faces a different tax burden as soon as the new "Internal Revenue Code of 1986" becomes fully effective. Because the Harris family has been well advised, a combination of losses from multifamily apartment and office building construction have enabled Joe, Tom and Harry to offset much of their income (derived from the sale of lots, the sale of single family homes and, for Joe, from the securities which he had originally purchased with his refinancing proceeds).

Passive Losses

Principally, because of the enactment of the new section 469 of the 1986 Internal Revenue Code, an entirely different tax result will be enforced. The objective of the new rule is to segregate and tax net portfolio income plus active income (such as income from lot and home sales) without offset by "passive losses." Such losses derive from any business in which the taxpayer does not "materially participate" and all income from rental activities (whether or not the taxpayer materially participates in that activity).* In addition, under no circumstance can income from portfolio investments, such as dividends, interest, annuities or royalties, be offset by passive losses. Accordingly, Joe's income from the investment of these refinancing proceeds will be subject to ordinary income tax as will, in the case of Joe, Tom and Harry, the income from lot sales, home sales, and the construction income derived by the Subchapter S corporations.

In further application of the passive loss rules, the "suspended losses" generated by the losses from office buildings and apartment houses (whether existing or newly constructed) can be used only if the Harris family generates "passive" income, i.e., income, other than portfolio income, from a realty or nonrealty limited partnership interest, or any active business in which neither Joe, Tom nor Harry materially participate. Such losses can, however, ultimately be realized if any of the properties which generate such losses are disposed of in a fully taxable transaction and, under certain circumstances, through application of possibly the "ultimate loop-hole," i.e., death.**

There is an exception to the passive loss limitation for smaller-scale investors (i.e., smaller than Harris Companies) in rental housing. Investors with incomes below $100,000 are allowed to offset up to $25,000 in non-passive income with such passive losses, provided they "actively participate." This exception phases out between $100,000 and $150,000 income. See Chapter 3 and the Appendix for a fuller discussion.

**The amount of suspended deductions which are allowable upon the death of a taxpayer are, however, severly limited. Under the passibe loss rules, only the excess of the amount of passive losses over the amount of "stepped-up" basis which occurs at deathis deductible. In many cases, where a depreciable structure, such as the warehouse, has been substantially or fully depreciated, the amount of the basis step-up will equal, or conceivably exceed, the amount of suspended passive losses (particularly with respect to buildings now on hand, where, because of the phase-in rules, the amount of suspended losses will be minimal). On the other hand, if a*

Closely Held C Corporations

The tax advisors also note that there are special opportunities, the benefits of which are limited to "closely held" C corporations (which are not Subchapter S corporations and which have 5 or fewer persons actually or constructively owning 50 percent or more of the stock). Unlike an individual or a shareholder in a Subchapter S corporation, closely-held C corporations enjoy special advantages since "active" income, such as management service activities or any other business income, can be utilized to offset passive losses. This is of interest because losses on real estate rentals, such as those realized by the Warehouse Corporation, always constitute passive losses whether or not the owner (i.e., the C corporation) "materially participates" in the management of the property. These losses will continue to be "wasted" at the Warehouse Corporation level unless they can be offset by appropriate forms of income.

Because of this, if Joe so desires, he can consider a nontaxable contribution of lot development land to the Warehouse Corporation, thereby generating ordinary income, the tax on which can be offset by the depreciation and interest from the operation of the warehouse which occurs at the C corporation level. If Joe has any immediate use for the profits he will be required to pay dividends subject in that case to ordinary income tax (at 38.5 percent in 1987 and 28 percent thereafter). Alternately, if he has no need to realize these profits, the C corporation can be held by him permanently (i.e., until death) and all of the shares transmitted to his wife and/or children without income tax on either the appreciation in the building or the profits (assuming they continue to be offset by losses from the Warehouse Corporation or new losses from other contributed appreciable realty, during his lifetime).

Subchapter S Corporations

Another possible means of limiting otherwise taxable income involves the Subchapter S corporations.* Consideration may be given to disbanding the HT Corporation and by entering into a "cost sharing" arrangement with each of the rental structures which are presently managed by the HT Corporation, by allocating the selling costs directly to the homes, and by entering into similar arrangements respecting the other Subchapter S corporations. Charges which would be omitted from the foregoing would be those costs referrable to the salaries of Tom and Harry as well as earnings otherwise taxable to them (thereby inflating the yield from the house sales and rental apartments in the form of reduced passive losses). Here again, caution must be exercised in the application of this approach pending publication of regulations under the passive loss provisions.

(cont'd) taxpayer dies under circumstances where a structure has been recently constructed, and he has already realized substantial "up front" losses (from initial depreciation and interest deductions) the amount of the loss may well exceed the basis step up. In that instance the excess of the suspended losses over the recent fair market value will be deductible.

* It should be noted that these entities are presently operating on a November 30 fiscal year. The new law requires that they adapt to a calendar year by including the deferred income over a four year period.

Appendix

PROVISIONS OF THE TAX REFORM ACT OF 1986 RELATED TO HOUSING

Floyd L. Williams
Tax Counsel, Government Affairs
National Association of Home Builders

OVERVIEW

Recently, the Congress of the United States enacted one of the most sweeping tax reform bills of this century. When fully implemented, the "Tax Reform Act of 1986" will have an impact upon virtually every individual taxpayer and business in this country. Between now and the time of implementation (generally, January 1, 1987), individuals and businesses, in particular, should reassess their current tax planning in order to take advantage of, or to mitigate their damage under, the new tax law.

This discussion focuses primarily upon the impact of tax reform on single-family and multifamily housing. References are made to the chapters in this guide which examine that business area or provision in greater detail.

SINGLE-FAMILY HOUSING

Homeowners (Chapters 1,8)

In large part, although there are some negative aspects of the new tax law, single-family housing has emerged as a "winner." This is because mortgage interest (on debt up to the purchase price plus the cost of improvements on up to two personal residences) remains fully deductible. Furthermore, real property taxes remain fully deductible. In addition, homeowners will still be able to avoid recognition of gain when they sell a home and move up to a more expensive home, and, if they are age 55 or older, they still can exclude from income up to $125,000 of gain on the sale of their principal residence.

One thing existing homeowners will want to watch out for is the denial of deductions for interest on consumer debt. This provision disallows, for example, interest deductions on debt incurred to purchase an auto or other consumer good. In order to prevent homeowners from avoiding the consumer interest restriction by tapping into their home equity and claiming additional mortgage interest deductions, the new law generally limits the mortgage interest deduction to debt on up to the purchase price of the home plus the cost of improvements. For example, assume that Mr. and Mrs. Brown purchased a home in 1977 for $100,000 and took back an $80,000 mortgage. Today, their home is worth $150,000 and they want to refinance in order to pull out some equity and to take advantage of the current low interest rates. Let's say they replace their existing mortgage with a $120,000 mortgage (80 percent of the home's current value). The Browns' use the proceeds from the refinancing to add a screened porch to the house, at a cost of $10,000, and use the remaining funds to buy a new car and take a trip to Europe. Their mortgage interest deduction will be limited to $110,000 of debt (that is, the original $100,000 cost plus the $10,000 improvement).

Debt incurred on or before August 16, 1986, and secured by the residence on August 16, 1986, is not subject to this new restriction. That is, if such debt exceeds the cost basis (purchase price plus improvements), then such amount is treated as the taxpayer's cost basis.

Notwithstanding this general limitation on mortgage interest deductions, home mortgage interest on debt in excess of the purchase price plus improvements, up to the fair market value of the residence, is fully deductible if the debt is incurred for educational or medical expenses.

Home Builders (Chapter 1)

While the tax benefits of homeownership are largely retained under the new law, certain homebuilders will be disadvantaged compared to current law. This is because of new restrictions on mortgage revenue bonds, a reduction (or, in some cases, elimination) of the benefits of the installment sales method of accounting, and the taxation of "contributions in aid of construction."

Mortgage Revenue Bonds. Mortgage revenue bonds have been a way to provide below market rate financing to moderate-income, first-time homebuyers. The new law restricts the issuance of mortgage revenue bonds in several ways:

* In general, 95 percent of bond proceeds must be used to provide loans to first-time home buyers;

* All loans generally must be made to persons having incomes of 115 percent or less of the higher of area or state median income; and

* The purchase price of a bond-financed residence generally may not exceed 90 percent of the average area purchase price applicable to that residence.

As important as the new restrictions is the fact that mortgage revenue bonds will be subject to a much more severe, annual State volume limitation. This volume limitation, which must be shared with a number of other non-governmental obligations, is the greater of $75 per resident or $250 million. One bright spot, however, is that mortgage revenue bonds have been extended through 1988. These changes generally apply to bonds issued after August 15, 1986.

Installment Sales. The changes made to the installment method of accounting will have their greatest impact on larger volume homebuilders who have been able to avail themselves of "builder bond" financing to provide relatively low interest rate financing to moderate income homebuyers. Under a builder bond program, the builder sells homes on the installment basis and takes back seller financing. The installment notes are then pledged to secure borrowed money that is used for new construction. The advantage of a builder bond program is that the builder can borrow money on which no tax is due while, at the same time, defer profit from new home sales.

Under the new law, the use of the installment method is disallowed generally to the extent of the builder's debt to equity ratio. Thus, if a builder is 100% leveraged, then all profit must be reported in the year of sale. Likewise, if a builder is 50 percent leveraged (i.e., debt represents 50 percent of total assets), then 50 percent of profit must be reported in the year of sale.

This provision generally applies to taxable years ending after December 31, 1986, with respect to sales after February 28, 1986. However, limited transitional relief is provided. (See Exhibit A.1 for more detail.)

Contributions in Aid of Construction. Under present law, when a builder contributes money or property to a regulated public utility company as an inducement for the utility to provide service (e.g., water, gas, or electricity), the utility does not have to pay tax on the money or property received. Under the new law, however, contributions in aid of construction made to a regulated public utility after December 31, 1986, will be treated as taxable income to the utility. This provision will increase builders' development costs, because non-municipal utilities now will seek additional money from the builders in order to satisfy the tax liability that results from a contribution in aid of construction. Furthermore, this provision will result in higher prices to homebuyers if builders choose to pass on these increased costs.

MULTIFAMILY HOUSING AND COMMERCIAL BUILDINGS

Builders of multifamily housing and commercial real estate will be affected much more adversely by the new tax law than will single-family homebuilders. This is because of provisions in the new law that:

* Substantially restrict the deduction of losses from "passive" activities;

* Limit the deduction of investment interest;

* Repeal the deduction for long-term capital gains;

* Substantially lengthen allowable depreciation lives;

* Repeal rapid amortization of construction period interest;

* Repeal rapid amortization of low-income housing rehabilitation expenses;

* Substantially restrict the issuance of multifamily industrial development bonds;

* Reduce the utility of the rehabilitation tax credit;

* Tighten the at-risk exception for real estate activities;

* Substantially strengthen the individual and corporate minimum taxes; and

* Reduce the benefit of installment sales treatment for sales of business or investment property.

Losses and Credits from Passive Activities (Chapters 2,3)

Rental real estate traditionally has been an attractive investment for several reasons, including rapid depreciation, the current deduction of interest expenses, and the availability of capital gains treatment on sale. By "leveraging" their investments through nonrecourse loans (i.e., generally loans secured by the property) individuals have been able to deduct currently losses substantially exceeding their out-of-pocket expenses. These losses then could be used to offset income (e.g., salaries, dividends, and interest income) unrelated to the real estate investment. Hence, the term "tax shelter." In addition to deferring current tax liability, individuals were able to "convert" ordinary income into capital gains on sale if straight-line depreciation was elected on residential rental property (i.e., for a top-bracket taxpayer, deductions produced tax savings of 50 percent at the margin, while gain on sale was taxed at only 20 percent). However, if accelerated depreciation was used, then gain on sale of residential rental property was taxed to the extent of the difference between actual depreciation and depreciation that would have been allowable under the straight-line method. In the case of commercial real estate, all prior depreciation was "recaptured" on sale, unless straight-line depreciation was used.

The new law substantially clamps down on the tax sheltering possibilities from investments in passive activities. Passive activities are those trade or business activities in which the taxpayer does not materially participate, and rental activities. Material participation generally requires regular, continuous, and substantial activity on the part of the taxpayer. For example, a limited partnership interest in an activity would not give rise to material participation. However, a "working interest" in oil and gas property generally would not be considered a passive activity.

Deductions from passive activities, to the extent they exceed income from passive activities (exclusive of portfolio income), generally may not be deducted against the taxpayer's other income (i.e., salary, dividends, and active business income). Assume a taxpayer has gross rental income of $10,000 and rental loss (arising from depreciation and interest deductions as well as operating expenses) of $20,000. If the taxpayer has no other passive activity income, then only $10,000 of the $20,000 loss could be deducted currently. However, if the taxpayer had at least an additional $10,000 of passive activity income (e.g., from a limited partnership interest in a cattle feeding venture or from another rental project), then the full $20,000 of loss could be deducted in the current year.

Similar to losses, credits from passive activities generally are limited to taxes allocable to income from passive activities. However, more liberal rules apply to the new low-income housing tax credit and the rehabilitation tax credit, both of which are discussed below.

Losses and credits that cannot be used in the current year (i.e., "suspended losses") are carried forward and treated as deductions and credits from passive activities in the next taxable year. Thus, for example, losses that have been disallowed in previous years may be claimed when a rental property begins to produce positive taxable income. When the taxpayer disposes of his or her entire interest in an activity, any remaining suspended loss incurred in connection with that activity is allowed in full. The suspended loss will be deducted first against income or gain from the passive activity (including gain on disposition), then against net income or gain from all passive activities, and finally against any other income or gain. Assume, for example, that after 5 years an individual has $50,000 of suspended losses with respect to an apartment building. Assume, further, that a sale of the building produces $100,000 of profit. The individual would report $50,000 of gain in the year of sale (i.e., $100,000 of profit minus $50,000 of suspended losses).

There is an exception to the general passive activity loss restrictions for certain individuals who are "active participants" in rental real estate activities. Active participation is a less stringent standard than material participation in that it does not require as much personal involvement. At a minimum, however, the individual must not be a limited partner and must possess at least a 10 percent interest in the property. The active participation standard can be satisfied without regular, continuous, and substantial involvement, so long as the taxpayer participates, for example, in the making of management decisions or arranging for others to provide services, in a significant and bona fide sense. Management decisions that would be relevant, for this purpose, include approval of new tenants, fixing of rental terms, approval of capital or repair expenditures, and other similar decisions.

An individual who meets this active participation standard may offset up to $25,000 of non-passive activity income (e.g., income from active businesses, salaries, and dividends and interest) by using losses and credits from rental real estate activities. The $25,000 amount is available only to taxpayers whose adjusted gross income does not exceed $100,000. This amount is reduced by 50 percent of the amount by which a taxpayer's adjusted gross income exceeds $100,000. Thus, a taxpayer with $150,000 or more of adjusted gross income for the year would not qualify for the active participation exception.

The passive loss restrictions generally apply to individuals (including partners and subchapter S corporation shareholders), estates, trusts, and personal service corporations. Because the restrictions do not apply to regular corporations, more corporations may invest in rental real estate in order to offset their active business income. Likewise, individuals who currently are heavily sheltered will be seeking passive activity income in order to be able to offset their losses.

The passive activity loss provision generally is effective for taxable years beginning after December 31, 1986. Thus, some individuals who made investments in previous years will begin to feel the pinch of the provision in 1987. However, the provision is phased in over a 5-year period for investments made on or before October 22, 1986. (i.e., the date on which the President signed the bill). During the phase-in period, the amount of excess losses and credits that are disallowed is limited to 35 percent in 1987, 60 percent in 1988, 80 percent in 1989, 90 percent in 1990, and 100 percent in 1991. For example, an individual will be permitted to take 65 percent of passive activity losses attributable to pre-enactment investments in 1987, without limit.

A special transition rule exempts certain low-income housing investors from the passive loss restrictions for up to seven years, if the investment was made in 1984, 1985, or 1986 and at least 50 percent of the payments are required to be made after

1986. (See Exhibit A.2 for more details.)

Investment Interest Deductions   (Chapter 3)

In general, the deduction for investment interest is limited to the amount of a taxpayer's net investment income for the year. (Under prior law, investment interest could offset net investment income plus $10,000.) Investment interest includes all interest on debt not incurred in connection with the taxpayer's trade or business (other than consumer interest and qualifying interest on the taxpayer's principal and second residence). Investment income includes gain on investment property, the taxpayer's share of income or loss attributable to any limited business interest that is not subject to the passive loss rules, and gross income from interest, dividends, rents, and royalties.

Interest that is incurred with respect to any activity that is subject to the passive loss rules is not treated as investment interest (but is subject to the passive loss rules).

The provision is phased in, effective for taxable years beginning after December 31, 1986. Interest that is disallowed under this provision becomes subject to disallowance of 35 percent in taxable years beginning in 1987, 60 percent in 1988, 80 percent in 1989, 90 percent in 1990, and 100 percent in 1991.

Capital Gains   (Chapters 2,7)

The new law repeals the deduction for net long-term capital gains of individuals. (As a result of the current 60 percent capital gains deduction, the top capital gains tax rate is 20 percent.) Under the new law, capital gains of individuals, estates, and trusts will not be taxed at rates higher than 28 percent in 1987 (however, in 1988 and later capital gains of some individuals will be taxed at 33 percent if they are in the income range at which the benefits of the 15-percent rate and personal exemptions phase out). Since this provision is effective for taxable years beginning after December 31, 1986, individuals who entered into installment sales in prior years will be taxed at higher rates on payments received after that date. Furthermore, since the new law does not change the character of gain as capital or ordinary, net capital losses will continue to offset only $3,000 of ordinary income.

Real Estate Depreciation   (Chapters 2,7)

The new law stretches out the current 19 year depreciable life for residential rental real estate to 27 1/2 years. Commercial buildings will be depreciated over a 31 1/2 year period. In both cases, only the straight-line method will be permitted and there will be no "recapture" of deductions on disposition.

Thus, for residential rental property placed in service after December 31, 1986, the depreciation recovery percentage will be approximately 3.6 percent a year. For commercial property, the recovery percentage will be approximately 3.2 percent. This amounts to a substantial reduction in the value of depreciation deductions, compared to present law. For example, assume a building with a cost of $10,000,000 is placed in service at the beginning of a year. The first year deduction would be $882,675, using 19-year accelerated depreciation, $504,386, using 19-year straight-line depreciation, $348,485, using 27 1/2-year straight-line depreciation, and $304,233, using 31 1/2-year straight-line depreciation.

Property that is constructed, reconstructed, or acquired pursuant to a written contract that was binding on March 1, 1986, may be depreciated over a 19-year period (15-years if low-income housing), provided the property is placed in service before January 1, 1991.

Construction Period Interest (Chapter 2)

Currently, interest that is paid or incurred on a construction period loan may be amortized and deducted ratably over a 10-year period. Under the new law, construction period interest must be capitalized (i.e., added to basis and recovered through depreciation) for real property either constructed or produced for resale or used in the taxpayer's business.

Because of this change in the treatment of construction period interest, increased attention should be given to keeping the construction period as short as possible.

At-Risk Rules (Chapter 3)

The at-risk rules, which currently do not apply to real estate, are intended to prevent a person from deducting losses in excess of actual economic investment in an activity. These rules will be extended to real estate acquired after 1986.

In general, an individual is considered at risk to the extent of cash contributions to the activity, the adjusted basis of other property contributed to the activity, and amounts borrowed for use in the activity with respect to which the individual has personal liability or has pledged property not used in the activity as security for repayment. However, an important exception to the at-risk rule is provided for qualified nonrecourse financing that is secured by real property used in the activity. In general, qualified nonrecourse financing is a loan from an unrelated person who is actively engaged in the business of lending money (e.g, a bank), who was not the former owner of the property, and who did not receive a fee with respect to the borrower's investment in the property. Furthermore, real estate joint ventures may obtain financing from an otherwise qualified lender who has an equity interest in the venture, provided that the terms of the financing are commercially reasonable and substantially similar to loans made to unrelated parties. This exception will permit non-recourse financing, for example, in real estate joint ventures between individuals and savings and loan associations where both have an equity interest in the venture. The qualified nonrecourse financing exception, however, does not extend to seller financing. This may prove to be a particular problem to banks attempting to sell foreclosure property.

Multifamily Industrial Development Bonds (Chapter 5)

The new law provides for a much deeper targeting of multifamily IDBs issued after August 15, 1986. Prior to August 6, multifamily IDBs could be issued to finance projects in which at least 20 percent of the units in a project were set aside for families earning 80 percent or less of median area income. The new targeting requirement is that at least 20 percent of the units must be set aside for families earning 50 percent or less of area median income, or, alternatively, at least 40 percent of the units must be set aside for families earning 60 percent or less of area median income; in both cases adjusted for family size.

In addition, the new law provides a unified State volume cap for all private activity bonds (including multifamily IDBs) except (1) qualified section 501(c)(3) bonds (e.g., hospital bonds); (2) bonds for governmentally-owned airports, docks, and wharves, (3) bonds for governmentally-owned solid waste disposal facilities, and (4) veterans' mortgage bonds. The unified volume cap for each State is the greater of $75 per resident or $250 million, until December 31, 1987, when the cap will be reduced to the greater of $50 per resident or $150 million. These changes generally apply to bonds issued after August 15, 1986.

Tax Credit for Investment in Low-Income Rental Housing (Chapter 6)

The new law provides a tax credit for owners of residential rental property providing low-income housing. This new tax credit replaces all existing incentives for investment in low-income housing (i.e., preferential depreciation, five-year amortization of rehabilitation expenditures, and special treatment of construction period interest and taxes).

Under the new law, a maximum credit of 9 percent each year for 10 years will be allowed on expenditures for new construction and rehabilitation of qualifying low-income housing units that are not Federally subsidized. A maximum credit of 4 percent each year for 10 years will be allowed on expenditures for new construction and rehabilitation financed with tax-exempt bonds or similar Federal subsidies (e.g., FmHA section 515 loans).

In addition, there will be a maximum credit of 4 percent each year for 10 years on the cost of acquisition of low-income housing units. In general, such property must not have been previously placed in service within 10 years. For the new construction and rehabilitation credit, expenditures must exceed $2,000 per low-income unit.

Each state is permitted to issue low-income housing tax credits in an amount equal to $1.25 per resident of the state. Only qualifying expenditures that are not financed with the proceeds of tax-exempt bonds must receive credit authority from the state. Furthermore, expenditures from tax-exempt bond financing that are eligible for the credit receive the credit without reducing a state's credit authority. At least 10 percent of the credit authority of each state must be reserved for projects that are developed by certain non-profit organizations, one of the exempt purposes of which is the fostering of low-income housing.

Credits (but not other losses) are treated as derived from property in which the owner actively participates (producing a maximum annual credit of $7,000 per investor). The income phase-out range for the credit is between $200,000 and $250,000. Thus, individuals earning more than $250,000 generally are not eligible for the credit.

One of the following targeting requirements must be met in order for a project to qualify:

* At least 20 percent of the units in the project must be occupied by individuals having incomes of 50% or less of area median income, adjusted for family size; or

* At least 40 percent of the units must be occupied by individuals having incomes of 60 percent or less of area median income, adjusted for family size.

The rent (including tenant-paid utilities) charged to tenants in units with respect to which the credit is allowable may not exceed 30 percent of the qualifying income. Eligible projects must satisfy these targeting requirements continuously for a 15-year period, otherwise a portion of the prior credits will be recaptured. The income limits may be adjusted for areas with unusually low family income or high housing costs relative to family income in a manner consistent with determinations of very-low-income families and area median gross income under section 8 to reflect the 50-percent and 60-percent income levels. The basis of a project, for depreciation purposes, is not reduced by the amount of the credit. However, if a historic rehabilitation credit also is claimed, the rehabilitation credit would reduce depreciable basis. The provision applies to property placed in service after December 31, 1986 and before January 1, 1990. Property placed in service after 1989 will be eligible for the credit if expenditures of 10 percent or more of total project costs are incurred before January 1, 1989, and the property is placed in service before January 1, 1991.

Rehabilitation Tax Credit (Chapter 7)

The new law replaces the existing three-tier rehabilitation credit with a two-tier credit for qualified rehabilitation expenses. For property placed in service after December 31, 1986, the historic rehabilitation credit will drop from 25 percent to 20 percent. Furthermore, the full rehabilitation expense, rather than 1/2, will have to be subtracted from the building's depreciable basis. A 10 percent credit will be allowed for rehabilitation of buildings placed in service before 1936. Up to $7,000 of credit (i.e., the credit equivalent of a $25,000 loss deduction) will be available as an exception to the passive loss limitation for investors with up to $200,000 of adjusted gross income (without regard to the passive loss limitation). For investors with more than $250,000 of adjusted gross income, the credit will be available only against tax generated from passive activities.

Individual Minimum Tax (Chapter 3)

The individual minimum tax rate is increased to 21 percent. Real property depreciation is a preference to the extent of the difference between 40-year straight-line depreciation and actual depreciation claimed for regular tax purposes. In general, interest on nonessential function tax-exempt bonds (other than section

501(1)(3) bonds) issued on or after August 8, 1986 is a preference item. The installment sales method of accounting is not allowed for purposes of the minimum tax computation. The passive loss limitation applies for purposes of the minimum tax. (The transition relief for pre-enactment investments does not apply for minimum tax purposes.) Untaxed appreciation on gifts of appreciated property is treated as a tax preference. The provision generally applies to taxable years beginning after December 31, 1986.

Corporate Minimum Tax (Chapter 3)

The corporate minimum tax rate is increased to 20 percent. The structure is generally the same as the individual minimum tax. A new preference is provided for 50 percent of the excess pre-tax book income over alternative minimum taxable income. The provision generally applies to taxable years beginning after December 31, 1986.

Installment Sales (Chapter 9)

The new law limits the use of the installment method based on the ratio of debt to assets for sales of real property used in a trade or business or held for the production of rental income, if the selling price of the property exceeds $150,000.

This provision can be illustrated by the following example: Assume a taxpayer sells rental property for $1 million profit on the installment basis (taking no down payment). Assume, further, that the taxpayer's total debt (including debt on the building) is $800,000 and that the taxpayer has assets (including the installment note) worth $2 million. The taxpayer would have to report $400,000 of the selling price as a payment in the year of sale.

(That is $\underline{\$800,000} \over \$2,000,000$ X $1,000,000 = $400,000.)

This provision is effective for taxable years ending after December 31, 1986, with respect to sales after August 16, 1986.

ITEMS OF GENERAL INTEREST

Individual Income Tax Provisions

Tax Rates. For taxable years beginning in 1987, a five-bracket rate schedule is provided:

Taxable Income Brackets

Tax rate	Married	Single
11%	0-$3,000	0-$1,800
15%	$3,000-$28,000	$1,800-$16,800
28%	$28,000-$45,000	$16,800-$27,000
35%	$45,000-$90,000	$27,000-$54,000
38.5%	Over $90,000	Over $54,000

For taxable years beginning in 1988, a two-bracket rate schedule is provided:

Tax rate	Married	Single
15%	0-$29,750	0-$17,850
28%	Over $29,750	Over $17,850

Rate Adjustment. Starting in 1988, the benefit of the 15 percent rate bracket will be phased out for taxpayers with taxable income above specified levels. The income tax liability of those taxpayers will be increased by 5 percent of taxable income within specified ranges.

For married individuals (joint returns), the rate adjustment will occur between $71,900 and $149,250 of taxable income. For single individuals, the rate adjustment will occur between $43,150 and $89,650 of taxable income.

Standard Deduction (Zero Bracket Amount). For taxable years beginning in 1987, the standard deduction will be $3,760 for married individuals and $2,540 for single individuals. For taxable years beginning in 1988, the standard deduction will be $5,000 for married individuals and $3,000 for single individuals.

Personal Exemptions. The personal exemption for each individual, the individual's spouse, and each eligible dependent is increased to $1,900 for 1987, $1,950 for 1988, and $2,000 for 1989.

Starting in 1988, the benefit of the personal exemption will be phased out for taxpayers having taxable income above specified levels. For those taxpayers, income tax liability will be increased by 5 percent of taxable income within certain ranges. This reduction in benefit of the personal exemption begins at the taxable income level at which the benefit of the 15 percent rate is totally phased out (i.e., $149,250 for married individuals in 1988). The benefit of each personal exemption is phased out over an income range of $10,920 in 1988. (For example, in 1988, for a married couple with two children, the benefit of the four personal exemptions would phase out over an income range of $43,680 and would be phased out completely at taxable income of $192,930.) In 1989, the benefit of each personal exemption will phase out over an income range of $11,200.

Two-Earner Deduction. The two-earner deduction is repealed effective for taxable years beginning on or after January 1, 1987.

Income Averaging. Income averaging is repealed effective for taxable years beginning on or after January 1, 1987.

Earned Income Credit. The earned income credit (available to eligible individuals with one or more children) is increased to 14 percent of the first $5,714 of earned income (maximum credit of $800). The credit phases out between $6,500 and $13,500 of income in 1987, and between $9,000 and $17,000 of income in 1988. In addition, employers will be required to notify employees whose wages are not subject to income tax withholding that they may be eligible for the refundable earned income credit.

However, this notice need not be given to employees whose wages are exempt from income tax withholding (e.g., high school or college students with summer jobs).

Unemployment Compensation. All unemployment compensation benefits received after December 31, 1986, in taxable years ending after that date will be includible in gross income.

Scholarships and Fellowships. In general, the income tax exclusion for scholarship and fellowship grants will be limited to "course-related" expenses of degree candidates (e.g., amounts for room and board will be included in income.)

Employee Awards. Employee awards of tangible personal property for length of service or safety achievement are excludible by the employee and deductible by the employer, to the extent that during the year the aggregate cost of awards to the same employee does not exceed $1,600 for all awards and $400 for all awards that are not qualified plan awards. De minimis fringe benefits and traditional retirement gifts continue to be excludible from income.

Itemized Deductions for State and Local Taxes. The itemized deduction for State and local sales taxes is repealed ffective for taxable years beginning on or after January 1, 1987. Furthermore, state, local, or foreign taxes (other than real property taxes) that are incurred in a trade or business (or investment activity) in connection with the acquisition or disposition of property are not deductible. Instead, those taxes are to be treated as a part of the cost of the property on acquisition or as a reduction in the amount realized on disposition.

Charitable Deduction for Nonitemizers. Repealed, effective January 1, 1987.

Medical Expense Deduction. The floor under the itemized medical expense deduction is increased from 5 percent to 7.5 percent of adjusted gross income effective for taxable years beginning on or after January 1, 1987. Furthermore, the law is clarified to reaffirm that the full costs of specified capital expenditures incurred to accommodate a personal residence to the needs of a physically handicapped individual constitute deductible medical expenditures.

Deductibility of Mortgage Interest and Taxes Allocable to Tax-free Allowances for Ministers and Military Personnel. A permanent rule is provided that ministers receiving excludable parsonage allowances, as well as military personnel receiving excludable military housing allowances, are not precluded from deducting mortgage interest or real property taxes on their residences.

Meals, Travel, and Entertainment Expenses. In general, the deduction for business meal expenses, including meals away from home, is reduced to 80 percent of the cost of the meal, effective for taxable years beginning on or after January 1, 1987. However, full deductibility is allowed in 1987 and 1988 for the cost of meals provided as an integral part of a qualified banquet meeting (i.e., a convention, seminar, annual meeting, or similar business meeting if the program includes a meal, more than 50 percent of the participants are away from home, there are at least 40 attendees, and the meal event includes a speaker). Similar to meals, the deduction for business entertainment is reduced to 80 percent of the cost of the entertainment. In addition, deductions for skyboxes are disallowed (1/3 disallowance in 1987, 2/3 disallowance in 1988, and full disallowance in 1989). The deduction for the cost of luxury water transportation is limited to twice the highest Federal per diem for travel in the U.S.

No deduction is allowed for the cost of travel that would be deductible only on the ground that the travel itself constitutes a form of education.

The new law also eliminates deductions for registration fees, travel and transportation costs, meal and lodging expenses, etc., incurred in connection with attending a convention, seminar, or similar meeting relating to investment, financial planning, or other income-production activities. However, this disallowance rule does not apply to expenses incurred by a taxpayer in attending a convention, seminar, sales meeting, or similar meeting relating to the taxpayer's trade or business.

Miscellaneous Itemized Deductions. In general, employee business expenses (other than reimbursed expenses) will be allowed only as an itemized deduction, subject to a 2 percent of adjusted gross income floor. Miscellaneous itemized deductions (e.g., investment counsel fees and tax preparation expenses) are also subject to this floor. Moving expense deductions will be allowed only as an itemized deduction. These changes are effective for taxable years beginning on or after January 1, 1987.

Home Office Expenses. The deduction for home office expenses is limited to the taxpayer's net income from the business, effective for taxable years beginning on or after January 1, 1987.

Political Contributions Credit. The political contributions tax credit is repealed, effective for taxable years beginning on or after January 1, 1987.

Corporate Tax Rates

Corporate income will be taxed under a three-bracket, graduated rate structure as follows:

Taxable income	Tax rate
$50,000 or less	15%
$50,000-$75,000	25%
Over $75,000	34%

Similar to the individual tax rate structure, there will be a phase out of the benefit of graduated rates for corporations. This phase out will occur through the imposition of an additional 5 percent tax (for a total of 39 percent) between $100,000 and $335,000 of taxable income. Thus, corporations with taxable income of $335,000 or more, in effect, will pay tax at a flat 34 percent rate. The new rate structure applies to taxable years beginning on or after July 1, 1987. Income in taxable years that include July 1, 1987, will be subject to blended rates. Corporate net capital gains taken into account on or after January 1, 1987, will be taxed at the regular corporate rates.

Dividend Exclusion for Individuals

The $100 dividends received exclusion for individuals is repealed, effective for taxable years beginning after December 31, 1986.

Liquidating Sales and Distributions of Property (Chapter 9)

Present law generally provides that a corporation recognizes no gain or loss on a distribution of its assets to shareholders in liquidation, or if certain conditions are met, on a liquidating sale of its assets.

In general, under the new law, gain or loss will be recognized by a corporation on a liquidating sale of its assets. Gain or loss also generally will be recognized on a liquidating distribution of assets as if the corporation had sold the assets to the distributee at fair market value. However, neither gain nor loss will be recognized with respect to any distribution of property by a corporation to the extent there is nonrecognition of gain or loss in a tax-free reorganization. The provision generally is effective for liquidating sales and distributions after July 31, 1986. However, several transition rules are provided, including one that does not apply the change to liquidations completed before January 1, 1987, and another which gives small, closely-held corporations an additional two years to liquidate.

Energy-Related Tax Credits

Residential Solar Energy Tax Credit. The individual tax credit for 40 percent of expenditures made before December 31, 1985, for up to $10,000 of solar energy source property, was allowed to expire. Unused credits at the end of 1985 may be carried forward through 1987.

Business Energy Tax Credits. The energy tax credit for solar energy property was extended at the rate of 15 percent in 1986, 12 percent in 1987, and 10 percent in 1988. The geothermal tax credit was extended at the rate of 15 percent in 1986 and 10 percent in 1987 and 1988. The tax credit for biomass energy property was extended at the rate of 15 percent in 1986 and 10 percent in 1987. The credit for ocean thermal property was extended at the rate of 15 percent through 1988.

Limitation on General Business Credit

Currently, the general business tax credit earned by a taxpayer can be used to reduce up to $25,000 of tax liability, plus 85 percent of tax liability in excess of $25,000.

The 85 percent limitation is reduced to 75 percent, effective for taxable years beginning after December 31, 1986.

Targeted Jobs Tax Credit

The targeted jobs tax credit is extended for three years (i.e., 1986, 1987, and 1988). However, the credit for first-year wages is reduced from 50 percent to 40 percent of the first $6,000 of wages. No credit will be allowed for second-year wages.

Information Reporting on Real Estate Transactions

Real estate transactions must be reported to the IRS, effective for transactions with respect to which closing on the contract occurs on or after January 1, 1987. The primary responsibility for reporting is on the person responsible for closing the transaction, including any title company or attorney who closes the transaction.

Tax-exempt Interest Reporting

Effective for taxable years beginning after December 31, 1986, taxpayers must report on their tax returns the amount of tax-exempt interest they receive during the year.

IRAs

Deductible IRA contributions are permitted if an individual or married couple has adjusted gross income (AGI) below a phaseout level, or if the individual (and spouse, if married) is not as active participant in an employer-maintained retirement plan. For an individual who is an active participant in an employer plan, the IRA deduction limit is reduced proportionately for AGI between $25,000 and $35,000. For married individuals, the IRA deduction limit is reduced proportionately for AGI between $40,000 and $50,000, if either spouse is an active participant in an employee plan.

Exhibit A.1

TRANSITION RELIEF FOR INSTALLMENT SALES

Under the conference report, use of the installment method for certain sales by persons who regularly sell real or personal property to customers in the ordinary course of their trade or business, and for certain sales of business or rental property, is limited based upon the amount of the taxpayer's outstanding indebtedness.

In general, this "proportionate disallowance" rule is effective for taxable years ending after December 31, 1986, with respect to sales of property after February 28, 1986.

Limited transition relief applies to dealers in real property (i.e., home builders home using "builder bond" financing). Under the transition rule, any gain attributable to allocable installment obligations that arise (or are deemed to arise) in the first taxable year of the taxpayer ending after December 31, 1986, is taken into account ratably over the three taxable years beginning with such first taxable year. (For example, assume a calendar year taxpayer with sales after February 28, 1986. One-third of the gain from sales after February 28, 1986 and before January 1, 1988 would be taken into account in 1987, one-third would be taken into account in 1988, and one-third would be taken into account in 1989.) For installment obligations arising in the second taxable year of the taxpayer ending after December 31, 1986, any such gain is taken into account ratably over the two taxable years beginning with such second taxable year.

For "non-dealer" sales of business or rental property, the proportionate disallowance rule is effective for taxable years ending after December 31, 1986, with respect to sales after August 16, 1986. No transition relief applies to these sales.

Exhibit A.2

LOW-INCOME HOUSING TRANSITION RULE

The conference report provides transition relief for low-income housing activities. In general, losses from certain investments after 1983 are "grandfathered" from the passive activity loss restrictions for a period of up to seven years from the date of the taxpayer's original investment. Specifically, any loss sustained by a "qualified investor" with respect to an interest in a "qualified low-income housing project" for any taxable year in the "relief period" is not treated as a passive activity loss.

Qualified Investor

In general, a qualified investor is a natural person who holds an interest in a qualified low-income housing project and who is required to make payments of 50% or more of the total original obligated investment for such interest after December 31, 1986. If the project was placed in service before August 16, 1986, the investor must have held an interest in the project on August 16, and must have made his initial investment after December 31, 1983. If the project is not placed in service before August 16, 1986, then the investor must hold an interest in the project on December 31, 1986. An investor will be treated as holding an interest on August 16, 1986, or December 31, 1986, if on such date he had a binding contract to purchase the interest.

Qualified Low-Income Housing Project

A project is a qualified low-income housing project if all of the following requirements are met:

* The project meets the requirements of clause (i), (ii), (iii), or (iv) of Internal Revenue Code section 1250 (a)(1)(B)** as of the date placed in service and for each taxable year thereafter beginning after 1986;

* The operator certifies to the Treasury Department that the project met the requirements of Code sec. 1250 (a)(1)(B) on the date of enactment (or, if later, when placed in service) and annually thereafter;

* The project is constructed or acquired pursuant to a binding written contract entered into on, or before, August 16, 1986; and

* The project is placed in service before January 1, 1989.

** Projects meeting the requirements of clauses (i),(ii), (iii), or (iv) of Code sec.1250 (a)(1)(B) include (1) projects insured under sec.221(d)(3) or 236 of the National Housing Act (or similar programs under State or local law); (2) projects subsidized under sec. 8 of the United States Housing Act of 1937; (3) property described in Code sec. 167(k) (i.e., property eligible for rapid amortization of low-income housing rehabilitation expenses); and (4) projects insured under Title V of the Housing Act of 1949.

Relief Period

The relief period for the transitional rule begins with the taxable year the investor made his initial investment and ends with whichever of the following is the earliest:

* The sixth year after the taxable year of initial investment;

* The first taxable year after the taxable year in which the investor is obligated to make his last investment; or

* The taxable year preceding the first taxable year for which the project ceased to be a qualified low-income housing project.

Special Rule for Rural Housing. The Budget Reconciliation Act amended the 1986 Tax Act to provide alternative transition relief for certain investments in rural low-income housing. Under this alternative rule, if all of the other requirements described above are met, transition relief is available (for up to five years after the date of initial investment) where the investor is required to make payments of 35% or more of the total original obligated investment for his interest after December 31, 1986. This alternative standard for transition relief is available for interests in qualified FmHA Sec. 515 low-income housing projects that are located in towns with populations of less than 10,000 and which are not part of a metropolitan statistical area. Additionally, for investors to qualify under this provision, at least one-half of the number of payments required with respect to the interest must remain to be paid after December 31, 1986.